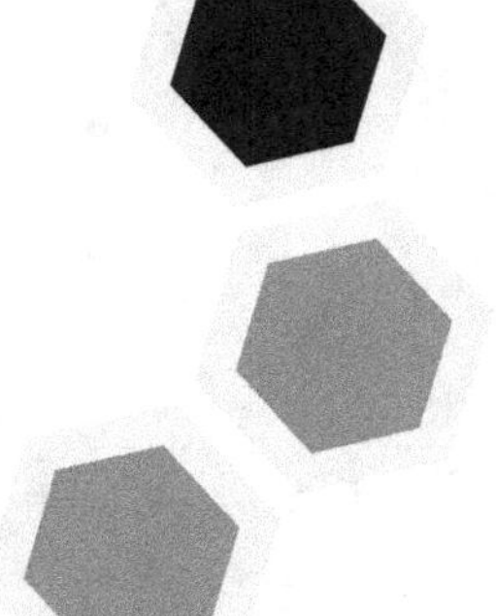

Cognitive Mechanics

Operations of the Mind

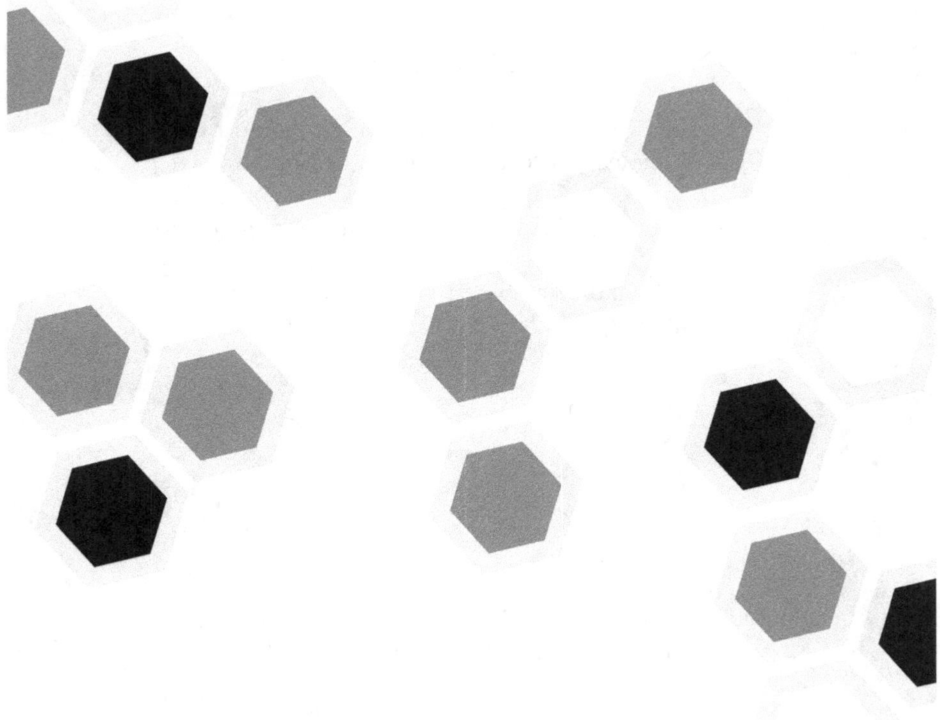

Ryan Williams

Cognitive Mechanics: Operations of the Mind

First Edition

ISBN: 9798496868129
Library of Congress Control Number: 2022904173

Visit us online at https://www.cognitivemechanics.org.

View and contribute to our source code at
https://github.com/CognitiveMechanics.

Special thanks to Kelsey Williams, for her efforts in designing
original graphics that appear throughout this work.

Thanks also to Anna Dean, for her insightful reviews and
feedback from the earliest stages of its production.

For my grandfather, Don Murray—
a delightfully curious man.

Cognitive Mechanics
Operations of the Mind

Ryan Williams

2022

Contents

Introduction

"In spite of the accumulation of detailed knowledge, how the human brain works is still profoundly mysterious."

— Francis Crick

After deconstructing cognitive functions into simple structures and operations, we will utilize them as material in rebuilding complex mental capabilities as conceptual machines.

I refer to this process of reverse and re-engineering the mind as *Cognitive Mechanics.*

Summary

If the mind were a machine, what would its components be? How would they interact? And can we reassemble these components into new machines with intelligent capabilities? This book attempts to build a framework to address these questions.

We can only expect this method of inquiry to take us so far; but I've found some surprise at the distance the mechanical approach has drawn me to this point.

The methods, structures, and general framework of this book come—in whole or in part—from a significant body of material I've gathered from others. I owe a great debt to the scientists, mathematicians, and engineers who built the many disciplines I put to use.

Outline

The basic trajectory of this book takes the following form, omitting a few interesting chapters that provide broader context and applications:

1. We describe states of the mind as hierarchical conceptual structures;
2. Based on our own experienced cognitive abilities, we propose a small set of fundamental operations on those structures;
3. We outline a method, termed *stratified analysis*, for expressing conceptual operations in terms of some lower-level (ostensibly physical) representation and vice versa;
4. We show that combinations of those simple operations can form into complex mechanisms by a process that essentially amounts to forming sets of conditionally-applied structural transformation rules;
5. We demonstrate a handful of specific machines that represent arithmetical hyperoperations (e.g. addition, multiplication, etc.);
6. We build a *universal conceptual machine*—a conceptual machine that can emulate any other conceptual machine—which gives us the ability to represent mechanisms as conceptual structures;
7. We define an operation that can gather similarities between conceptual structures;
8. We plausibly allude to how we might use that operation to extract the common states of arithmetical machines, formulated as conceptual structures to be evaluated by the universal machine;
9. Finally, we use those common structures to build a machine that can construct new machines to execute arbitrary hyperoperations.

This course illuminates a method for building machines that can learn from and generalize other machines. The book concludes with a sketch of such an "intelligent" machine, and sets in place a program to obtain that goal.

Computer Simulations

In the course of writing this book, I created a programming framework for simulating the conceptual structures and machines that are described within.

These simulations were a useful tool in debugging and verifying that the machines I wrote into the book actually worked. I expect to put them to further use in experiments related to language, learning, perceptual representations, and more.

To view the code or contribute, you can visit us on GitHub at https://github.com/CognitiveMechanics.

Visit Us Online

For up-to-date *Cognitive Mechanics* news and free articles, visit us online at https://www.CognitiveMechanics.org.

Syntax Reference

Below is a reference for the syntax used in the formal descriptions in this work. These are derived largely from formal logic and set theory, with a few unique forms specific to our system:

Syntax	Read As	Description
a	"Concept a"	Lowercase Latin letters are variables that represent *concepts*
α	"Perception *alpha*"	Lowercase Greek letters are used to represent *perceptions*
"thing"	"The word *thing*"	Words surrounded by quotes are sometimes used to represent the *word itself*, or the visual or auditory perception depicted by the word, as opposed to its actual meaning
‹thing›	"Perception of *thing*"	Words surrounded by single angle quotes are *perceptions* represented by the words
«thing»	"Concept of *thing*"	Words surrounded by double angle quotes are *concepts* represented by the words
$\langle a, b \rangle$	"Concept of composed of a and b"	The concept *composed of* a and b, via operation C (defined in detail in §2.2.6)
[thing]	"Component class *thing*"	Words surrounded by square brackets are *component classes* (defined in detail in §8.2.1)
$O(a, b) \rightarrow c$	"Operation O of a and b yields c"	Uppercase Latin letters followed by parenthesized arguments represent cognitive *operations*; see §2 for their full semantics
$O(a \mid b) \rightarrow c$	"Operation O of a with respect to b yields c"	The $\mid$ indicates an operation on a, with reference to b
$A \Rightarrow B$	"A implies B"	Logical implication; A implies B; if A therefore B

Syntax	Read As	Description
$A \Leftrightarrow B$	"A means the same thing as B"	Mutual implication; A implies B and vice versa; A if and only if B
$\Omega(a, b)$	"Predicate *Omega* of a and b"	Uppercase Greek letters followed by parenthesis indicate some relationship or property of their arguments; they have the values *true* or *false*
$\sigma(a, b)$	"Specifier *sigma* of a and b"	Lowercase Greek letters followed by parenthesis indicate a *concept* which has properties of its arguments; their semantics will always be defined before use
$a : \Omega(a), \Pi(a)$	"a such that *Omega a, Pi a*"	a has the properties Σ and Π
$a \wedge b$	"a and b"	Logical *and*
$a \vee b$	"a or b"	Logical *or* (inclusive)
$\neg a$	"not a"	Logical *not*
$a \equiv b$	"a is defined as b"	Used to define terms
$\{a, b\}$	"Set of a and b"	Sets are used in their set theory sense, an unordered collection of objects uniquely identifed by their specific set of members; sets can have any number of members
S	"Set S"	Uppercase Latin letters, particularly S are used as variables for sets
$\{a_{S_0}, b_{S_1}\}$	"A set *indexed* by S"	Indexed sets use another set to reference their members. In the above example a is indexed by the zeroth element of set S and b is indexed by S_1, etc.
$\{v(s)\}_{s \in S}$	"A set *indexed* by s in S"	Another set indexed by S; the value $v(s)$ is given each element s in S to build the set

Syntax	Read As	Description
$\{\}$	"empty set"	The set with no members
$\emptyset$	"null concept"	A concept that represents no result from operation X
$x \in Y$	"x in Y"	Indicates that x is a member of set Y
$x \notin Y$	"x not in Y"	Indicates that x is *not* a member of set Y
$\exists x \Omega(x)$	"there exists x where *Omega x*"	Used to indicate existence of an x that satisfies *Omega*
$\forall x$	"for all x"	States that the following applies to all x
$A \subseteq B$	"A is a subset of B"	Each element of set A exists in set B: $\forall x, x \in A \Rightarrow x \in B$
$A \cup B$	"union of A and B"	The set that contains all members of A and B
$A \cap B$	"intersection of A and B"	The set that contains all members of *both A and B*
$A \times B$	"Cartesian product of A and B"	A set of pairs $\{(a, b)\}_{\forall a \in A, \forall b \in B}$; every combination of the elements of A and B
$\mathcal{P}(A)$	"powerset of A"	The set of all potential subsets of A, including the empty set
$A \setminus B$	"difference of A and B"	The set that contains all members of A that are *not* in B
$\top$	"true"	True
$\bot$	"false"	False

Note first that *operations*, denoted by $\to$, are distinguished from *logical implication*, denoted by $\Rightarrow$, in that operations are processes that occur in time, whereas *logical implication* is an unqualified statement about the conditions preceding and succeeding the arrow. A full explanation of their semantics and usage will be outlined in §2.

Note also that "thing" is distinguished from ⟨thing⟩ in that "thing" is used to mean the actual visual characters or auditory phonemes of the word "thing," ⟨thing⟩ might be used to indicate that you see a *thing*.

Index of Defined Symbols

Throughout the work we will define a number of *operations, predicates, functions, quantifiers,* and *specifiers,* listed below:

Symbol	Name	Defined	Description
$C(\{a, ...\}) \to b$	*Construct* or *Compose*	§2.2.6	Creates a new concept
$E(a) \to \{b, ...\}$	*Enumerate*	§2.2.7	Enumerates a concept's *components*
$G(\{\alpha, ...\}) \to b$	*Generalize*	§7.2.3	Generalizes a concept from a set of mental entities
$I(a) \to b$	*Interpret*	§5.4.2	Interprets a perception into a concept
$K(\{\alpha, ...\})$	*Collect*	§6.2.2	The concept or perception that is manifested in a set of *correlates*
$L(a \mid b) \to a'$	*Learn*	§10.2.2	Learns by associating one concept with another
$M(\alpha)$	*Manifest*	§6.2.1	The set of *correlates* that is equivalent to a concept
$\mathcal{M}$	*Machine*	§12.2.18	A set of conceptual structures that acts as an automaton
$Q(a)$	*Productivity*	§3.2.2	Productivity of a concept
$R(a) \to b$	*Recount*	§2.4.12	Recounts related concepts
$S(a) \to b$	*Symbolize*	§17.1.7	Symbolizes a concept linguistically
$T(a, r, b) \to a'$	*Transclude*	§8.5.4	Substitutes one concept into another
$U(s, c) \to r$	*Universal*	§19.12.2	Executes a set of configurations c on state s to yield result r
$X(a, r) \to b$	*Extract*	§8.6.2	Extracts a concept from another
$W(\{a, ...\}) \to b$	*Withdraw*	§20.2.1	Withdraws an abstraction from a set of concepts

Symbol	Name	Defined	Description
$Y(a, r) \to b$	*Match*	§8.4.12	Yields a truth value for whether one concept matches the structure of another
h_x	*h-level*	§3.2.6	Used for *partial-quantification* of productivity values
$\Upsilon(a, b)$	*Upsilon*	§8.4.4	Indicates that one concept *matches* another
$\Upsilon^*(a|b)$	*Upsilon-Star*	§20.1.28	Returns a numerical metric of the information difference between concepts
$\Phi(a, b)$	*Relation* or *Phi*	§2.4.4	Indicates a relation between two concepts
$\Phi'(\{a, b\})$	*Phi-Prime*	§2.4.7	Indicates a set of relations between a set of concepts
$\Phi^*(b \mid a)$	*Phi-Star*	§7.4.11	Gives the probability of transition from one state to another
$\sigma(a, b)$	*Sigma* or *Sigma Specifier*	§12.2.3	A specifier that constructs a machine state
$\kappa(a)$	*Kappa* or *Key Specifier*	§11.5.4	A specifier that indicates a concept is being used as a *key*
$\epsilon(s, o)$	*Epsilon* or *Eval Specifier*	§19.5.1	A specifier that indicates an operation to be evaluated within a *universal conceptual machine*
$\rho(a)$	*Rho* or *Ref Specifier*	§19.4.2	A specifier that indicates a *ref* in a *universal conceptual machine*
$[\,]$	*Proxy*	§8.2.8	A placeholder concept which matches any concept
$[\cdot]$	*Dot proxy*	§8.4.7	A concept which matches exactly the *proxy* only

Index of Defined Terms

Below are listed the meaning and locations of defined terms:

Term	Defined	Definition
Partially-Quantified	§3.2.7	The property of a given productivity value that its denominator is an *h-level*
Perception	§5.1.2	A specific sensation as made available to the conceptual system
Primitive Concept	§7.1.1	A concept whose only component is itself
Productivity	§3.2.2	The utility of a concept
Ref	§19.4.2	A concept used in a universal machine that refers to the current emulated machine state
Related Concept	§2.4.1	A concept that may arise as a consequence of another
Tag	§8.2.8	The semantic concept in a component class
Universal Conceptual Machine	§19.1	A conceptual machine that can emulate any other conceptual machine

1 Concepts

"It seems that the human mind has first to construct forms independently before we can find them in things."

— Albert Einstein

The words I write here (and you read) have some form of life within them, deeper than the shapes of the letters on the page, or the sounds they evoke in our minds. We begin our exploration by examining *concepts*—the structures that lie beneath the words.

1.1 The Constituents of Meaning

1.1.1 – Most words function as labels that we assign to mental constructions. The label is the *word*. The mental construction is the *concept*.

1.1.2 – Concepts are the constituents of meaning.

1.1.3 – Let's take the concept «table». When I think about what a «table» is, I have images in my mind of different tables. I think about common features of tables, such as legs and tabletops. I think about words that describe a table. "A piece of furniture with a raised platform." I think about what a table is used for, as for writing or eating. I think about how the table I sit at now feels against my forearms, and the sound it might make if I were to knock on it.

1.1.4 – These thoughts are all *aspects* of my concept «table». My concept «table» is a generalization of all of those things.

1.1.5 – One type of conceptual *aspect* is a *component*. Concepts are *composed* of their *components*.

1.1.6 – The components of concepts are also concepts. A concept is either composed of other concepts, or it is composed only of itself.

1.1.7 – Not all concepts can be described with a single word. This is often the case due only to the occasional inadequacy of our vocabulary.

1.1.8 – For any clearly held concept, we can always invent a new word to serve as its label.

1.1.9 – Notice that although I think of the concept «table» as unitary, there are many concepts which make it up.

1.1.10 – There are also many possible instances of the concept «table». And it may be that there is no single quality that every thing I would describe as a "table" possesses.

1.1.11 – For example, almost all tables have legs. But some desks do not have legs, and have extended vertical surfaces that support them instead. My concept of «desk» is positively a type of «table».

1.1.12 – Concepts are not the same as any thing in the world. The concept of a table involves a group of other concepts. But no concept in that group, nor the group itself, maps perfectly to any «table» that actually exists somewhere.

1.1.13 – No concept is a perfect proxy to reality. Concepts are better seen in terms of analogy.

1.1.14 – My concept «black» is to the concept «table» in «black table» something like the stuff that makes up what I call the "table" is to the physical property of reflecting a minimal amount of light in the wavelengths visible to humans, i.e. what I call "black."

1.1.15 – Concepts are not only of objects. Concepts can be of actions, relationships, transformations, and properties, and of their combinations.

1.1.16 – «black» is a concept. «table» is a concept. «the black table» is a concept. «falling over» is a concept. «the black table fell over» is a concept.

1.2 Understanding

1.2.1 – My concept «table» is unique to me, but I operate with the idea that your concept «table»—though slightly different from my own—is similar enough that when I put the word "table" into use, I expect that we will converge on the same understanding.

1.2.2 – That understanding is embodied in the structure of the concept: in its components as well as its relationships to other concepts.

1.2.3 – Not just between people, but even in the same person at a different time, the experienced representation of a concept will be slightly different the next time it is recalled. For example, maybe next time the recalled «table» is a mahogany color instead of oak.

1.3 Lost Words

1.3.1 – When we are searching for a word, we know it's "there," but we can't find the right label. We grasp aspects of a specific concept that is related to the word, but not the word itself.

1.3.2 – Other words with similar meanings, or aspects of their meanings, go through your head. "It's like baseball, but British... And they play it in India... They have this thing called a wicket... I think it sounds like wicket..."

1.3.3 – Eventually, it comes to you: "Ah, *cricket*..."

1.3.4 – You know there's *something* there—are certain of it—and you can tell someone aspects of it; but you cannot think of one specific *aspect* of it. That aspect is the linguistic *label* for it—a *word*.

1.3.5 – This shows that there *must be* something like what we call a concept, which is not the same as the word or its other associated *aspects*. They are present in the mind and can be retrieved via other concepts that they are related to, even when the symbol (i.e. the word) is not available.

1.3.6 – The concept «cricket» is not one thing; it is a relationship between a number of different concepts: concepts of the «pitch», the «ball», the «paddle», the «players». We will see later, every concept's relations ultimately tie back to *primitive concepts*—and ultimately, to *perceptions*.

1.4 Abstractions

1.4.1 – An *abstraction* is a construction which models multiple things, or aspects of things, as a single thing. The single thing is the abstraction.

1.4.2 – All concepts are *abstractions*.

1.4.3 – Concepts are idealized and abstract forms. Even when I look at a specific table, the one in front of me, the concept in my mind of this particular table is not the same as the table itself.

1.4.4 – I do not have a perfect picture of every molecule that I deem to be part of the «table», or which are right next to the table but I consider part of the «air». I do not have a picture of exactly what the legs look like, or the pattern of the wood—just close enough that I could pick it out under many circumstances, if I were to perceive it again.

1.4.5 – In forming concepts, our minds "smooth out" and simplify the actual state of affairs in the world. We discard information and distill down a set of related mental entities into a single *concept*.

1.4.6 – The resulting concept does not have a one-to-one mapping to any feature or set of features within the world.

1.4.7 – Let's consider the concept «hill». I have seen many «hills» of various shapes and sizes. When we use the concept «hill», we are not referring to one thing, but to a set of examples, relations, and properties (i.e. other concepts), which all or some «hills» have in common.

1.4.8 – But that is not the only way in which a concept is an abstraction. Concepts are also abstractions in the sense that when we derive the concept from aspects of the world known to us through our senses, we take what are actually separate aspects of the world and refer to them as a single entity.

1.4.9 – This is the essence of our capability of object discrimination. We perceive objects—abstractions of sensations. Then we form them into concepts—abstractions of perceptions. In this way, conceptualization is a meta-version of our ability for object discrimination.

1.4.10 – Take as an example the tall grass on one side of the «hill», and the uprooted tree on the other. When we say "that hill" we are referring to many aspects of the «hill»—many of which are not even known specifically—and yet are contained in our concept «that hill».

1.4.11 – Suppose I am standing on the south side of a hill, and you show me a tree on the north side that I did not previously know was there. If you ask me: "Is this tree a part of the hill?" I will say: "Yes"—with no doubt in my mind that it *is* a part of my conceived «hill».

1.4.12 – «that hill» may drastically change over time, but it still retains its conceptualization as «that hill».

1.4.13 – From one season to another, «that hill» may become nearly unrecognizable, but it is still «that hill».

1.4.14 – We experience the world, and our own mind determines *subconsciously* what its objects will be. We perceive those objects, and our mind determines, *consciously or subconsciously*, what its concepts will be.

1.4.15 – Suppose I say, "That thing over there *is* a 'cabinet.'" I am either making a statement about what my concept «cabinet» is, or I expect the recipient must first have some idea about what my concept «cabinet» might be to understand what I say.

1.4.16 – This shows that the "*is-a*" relationship—the relationship between aspects of the world and our concepts of them—is not a property of the world. It is an application of the mind.

2 Operations

"What a peculiar privilege has this little agitation of the brain which we call 'thought.'"

— David Hume

With our notion of *concepts* in place, we can now put them to use. In this chapter, we define the basic cognitive operations on concepts, and establish the foundation for the structures and formal descriptions we develop throughout our exploration.

2.1 Definition & Semantics

2.1.1 – An *operation* represents a process of the mind or of the world. It exists temporally extended: it occurs over time.

2.1.2 – An operation takes a set of mental entities (e.g. *concepts*) and produces a new set of mental entities; the inputs and outputs of operations are mental entities.

2.1.3 – We use uppercase Latin letters to represent operations, and lowercase Latin letters to represent concepts.

2.1.4 – The operation O below is said to take a and b as *arguments*, and to *yield* its *product* c:

$$O(a,b) \to c$$

2.1.5 – This operation is defined as a process which *may* occur if given a and b, but it is not *required* to occur any time a and b are given.

2.1.6 – Operations can be chained together in sequence when the output of one provides the input of another.

2.1.7 – For example, when:

$$O_1(a) \to b$$

$$O_2(b) \to c$$

2.1.8 – Transitively, this implies:

$$O_1(a) \to c$$

2.1.9 – We may define anonymous operations:

$$(a,b) \to c$$

2.1.10 – Most simply, a conversion from a to b:

$$a \to b$$

2.1.11 – All named operations are broadly speaking identical to their anonymous counterpart, when all constraints are taken into account. At the conceptual level of description, they give the exact same results.[1]

$$O(a, b) \to c \equiv (a, b) \to c$$

2.1.12 – Once an operation is defined, we are able to substitute its yielded *product* anywhere the operation occurs in our descriptions.

2.1.13 – For example, if we are given:

$$O_1(a, b) \to c$$

2.1.14 – c can be substituted for $O_1(a, b)$ in the expression $O_2(O_1(a, b))$ to yield $O_2(c)$:

$$O_2(O_1(a, b)) \to O_2(c)$$

2.1.15 – But the inverse is *not* allowed; you *cannot* substitute $O_1(a, b)$ for c:

$$O_3(c) \nrightarrow O_3(O_1(a, b))$$

2.1.16 – Finally, any set may undergo a conversion to yield any of its members:

$$\{a, ...\} \to a$$

2.1.17 – Or any subset of its members:

$$\{a, b, c\} \to \{a, b\}$$

---

[1] Usually, a named operation also has a separate description at the level of the *manifestations*, which in many cases may mean that while two operations have identical signatures at the conceptual level, they operate differently at this lower level. This will be explained in greater detail in §6.

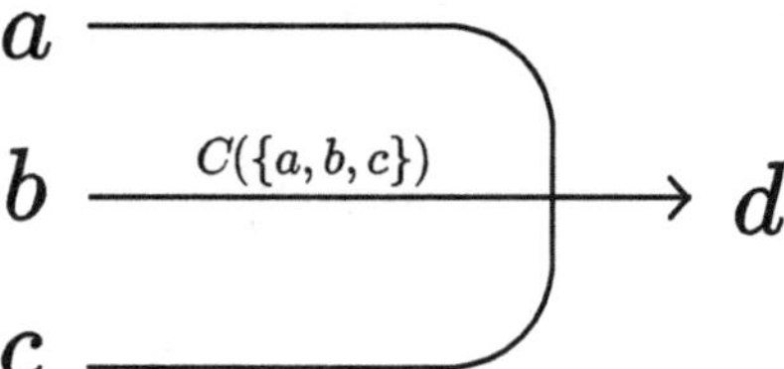

Figure 1: *Construction*: Concept d is *constructed* from its *component* concepts a, b, and c.

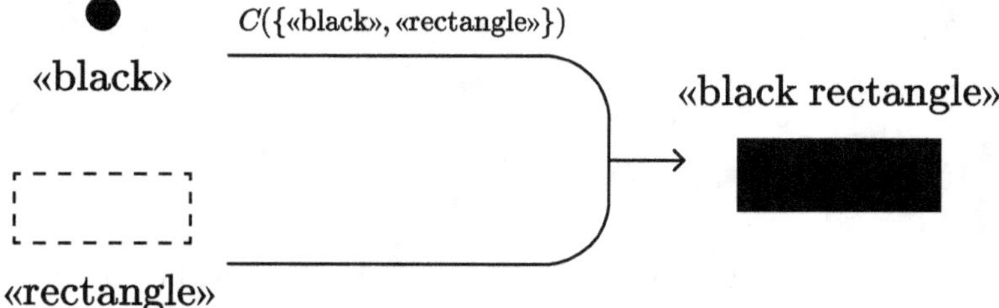

Figure 2: *Construction Illustrated*: The «black rectangle» is constructed from «black» and «rectangle».

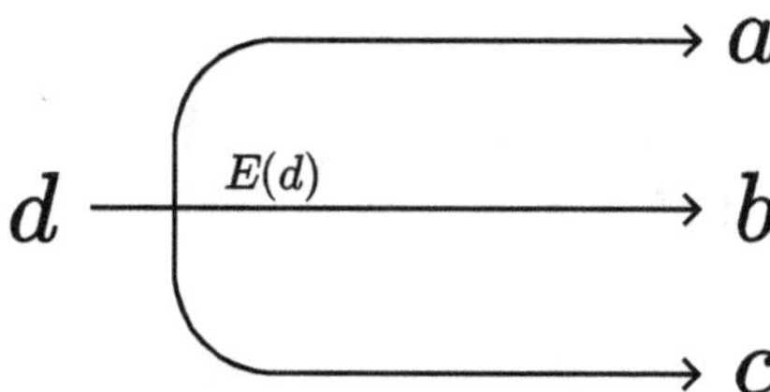

Figure 3: *Enumeration*: When concept d is *enumerated*, the operation yields its *component* concepts a, b, and c.

2.2 Construction & Enumeration

2.2.1 – When the Indigenous Americans of the Great Plains first encountered horses they referred to them as "big dogs."[2]

2.2.2 – The natives found them easy to domesticate, as they did their dogs—and accordingly used them for tasks similar to those dogs traditionally served, such as for modes of transport for their supplies when they periodically moved their settlements.[3]

2.2.3 – But though the horses shared *aspects* with their concept «dog», the Natives knew they were not dogs.

2.2.4 – They developed a concept of a «horse» before they had a specific word with which to converse about them. And in many cases, that word remained the equivalent of "big dog." Their concept was constructed as a composition of aspects of their concept «dog», with additional concepts—including «big».

2.2.5 – This is an important feature of concepts. They can undergo an operation to combine one or more *component* concepts to form a new concept.

2.2.6 – Below we define an operation C (*construct* or *compose*—used interchangeably), which takes a set of one or more concepts $\{a, ...\}$ and yields a new concept b.

$$C(\{a, ...\}) \to b$$

2.2.7 – The inverse of C is the operation E (as in *enumerate*).

2.2.8 – E takes the same concept b and yields its set of *components* $\{a, ...\}$.

$$E(b) \to \{a, ...\}$$

2.2.9 – Our capability to perform these operations is available to us subjectively.

2.2.10 – We can *construct* new concepts without having any new experience or perception.

---

[2] See Brown (1999), p29.

[3] Interestingly, the natives encountered feral horses, which arrived some years ahead of the European settlers traveling Westward—likely from whom the animals had escaped: see Haines (1928), p112.

2.3 Domain

2.3.1 – Concepts that have different roles can be *constructed*. For example, I can picture a «blue pentagon».

2.3.2 – The «blue pentagon» shares aspects with my concept «blue» and with my concept «pentagon».

2.3.3 – I am able to do this even if I have never seen or pictured a «blue pentagon» before.

2.3.4 – We are able to do this because «blue» and «pentagon» have no conflicting properties—one holding the role of the «color» and the other holding the role of the «shape».

2.3.5 – We call this "role," the set of potential usages of a concept, its *domain*.

2.4 Relations & Recountation

2.4.1 – Another type of conceptual *aspect* is a *relation* or a *related concept*.

2.4.2 – We know from our own experience that when we bring to mind one concept, it can readily bring our minds to other *related* concepts.

2.4.3 – When I think of «wood», I naturally think next of «trees», «acorns», «squirrels», «chirping», etc.

2.4.4 – We use Φ to indicate a *relation* between two concepts. We will use uppercase Greek letters to represent predicates about concepts. $\Phi(a, b)$ below represents the relation of concept a to concept b.

$$\Phi(a, b)$$

2.4.5 – Relations are *not* transitive. The relation of a to b is not the same as the relation of b to a. We know this because the strength of the relation from one concept to bring to mind another can be stronger in one direction than the other, say for the proclivity for my concept «brown» to evoke «tree bark», versus the opposite, «tree bark» to evoke «brown».

$$\Phi(a, b) \neq \Phi(b, a)$$

2.4.6 – In practice relations are generally bidirectional, and include sets of related items.

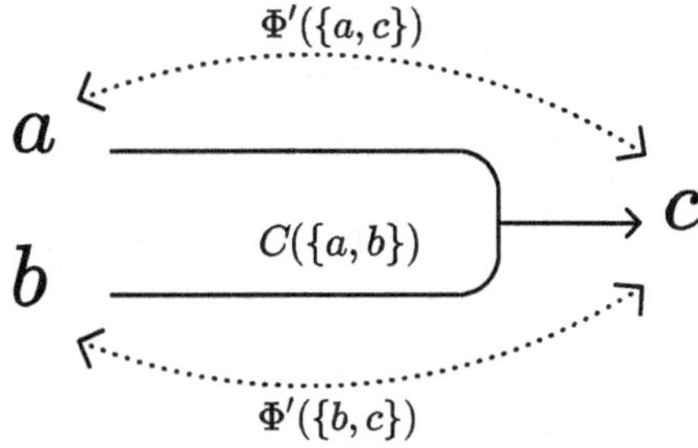

Figure 4: *Relation*: Concepts hold *relations* to their components. Pictured above, c hold relations to b and to a, and vice versa. These relations are indicated by the notations $\Phi'(\{a,c\})$ and $\Phi'(\{b,c\})$.

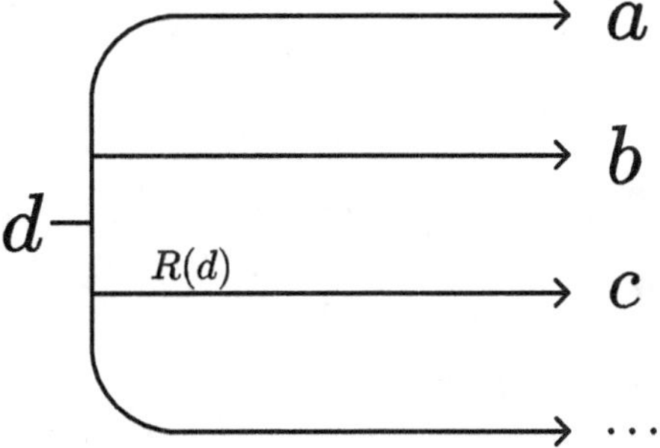

Figure 5: *Recountation*: *Recountation* lists related concepts. Above, concept d holds relations to a, b, c, and others, which are yielded by operation $R(d)$.

2.4.7 – For brevity, we will define Φ' which will take a set of concepts S and will denote every possible relationship between all members of S.[4]

$$\Phi'(S) \equiv \forall x \in S, \forall y \in S(\Phi(x,y) : x \neq y)$$

2.4.8 – For example, all possible relations between a, b, and c:

$$\Phi'(\{a,b,c\}) = \Phi(a,b) \wedge \Phi(b,a) \wedge \Phi(a,c) \wedge \Phi(c,a) \wedge \Phi(b,c) \wedge \Phi(c,b)$$

2.4.9 – When a new concept is constructed, it naturally retains relations to the concepts it was constructed from, and the component concepts obtain a new relation to the constructed concept.

$$C(a,b) \to c : \Phi'(\{a,c\}) \wedge \Phi'(\{a,b\})$$
$$C(c) \to d : \Phi'(\{c,d\})$$

2.4.10 – Relations of concepts can form bridges between concepts so that additional direct relations can be formed between them.

2.4.11 – Therefore, based on the above, potentially:

$$\Phi'(\{a,b,c,d\})$$

2.4.12 – A subset of a concept's *related* concepts can be *recounted* via the operation R.

$$R(c) \to \{\forall x_i : \Phi(c,x_i)\}$$
$$x_i \in R(c) \Leftrightarrow \Phi(c,x_i)$$

---

[4]Φ' does not represent a postulated relationship of the mind—it is for notational convenience only.

3 Productivity

"Truth is ever to be found in simplicity, and not in the multiplicity and confusion of things."

— Isaac Newton

What lends us to prefer one conceptual structure over another? Why do we apply the honorifics "true" and "real" to some, and dismiss others as "false?" In the chapter following, we define a pragmatic notion of *productivity*, the grounds for our tendency towards certain conceptual structures over others.

3.1 Productivity

3.1.1 – Concepts undergo a selection process. We tend to continue and increase our usage of concepts that we find useful, and to discontinue or decrease our usage of concepts that we do not find useful.

3.1.2 – We call the quality of being useful *productivity*.

3.1.3 – Although concepts may hold some analogy to states of affairs perceived external to the mind, the concept itself is *internal* to the mind—and its relations are to other mental entities.

3.1.4 – The boundaries of a concept are defined by the mind, hopefully in a way that will lead to *productive* uses.

3.1.5 – For example, there is nothing about the arrangement of atoms in a baseball that make the molecules within the baseball part of the baseball, and the molecules of air right next to them *not* part of the baseball.

3.1.6 – We use the concept «baseball» to refer roughly to a set of atoms in a particular configuration, because they tend to travel around the physical world together. Thus, the concept of «baseball» can lead to *productive* usage.

3.1.7 – To put it another way, a baseball is a «baseball» not because of something that is a part of its nature, but because we impose that description on particular forms of matter. We continue to impose that description on similar features of the world, because it is useful (i.e. *productive*) to us.

3.1.8 – Most ways of conceptualizing the world would result in a simple catalog of relations. Others conceptual structures are productive, and produce more utility than is contained within each of them do separately in and of themselves. This second kind is the one that we tend to continue our use of.

3.2 Productivity Algebra

3.2.1 – We will represent productivity using fractional quantities, but they will often be a special sort of fractions.

3.2.2 – We will use the notation $Q(x)$ to represent the *productivity* of a concept x, where n is the measure of productivity and h is the total measure of *possible* productivity.

$$Q(x) = \frac{n}{h} \;:\; n \leq h$$

3.2.3 – If we have a measure of what a perfect level of productivity would be, we can represent productivity with a value between 0 and 1.

3.2.4 – If we do not have a measure of what perfect productivity will be, we can express values such as $\frac{1}{h_0}$, $\frac{2}{h_1}$, $\frac{3.14159}{h_1}$, $\frac{1}{h_8}$, etc., where we understand h_0 to be a hypothetical denominator that operates as an initial point of reference.

3.2.5 – If a fundamental shift is made that results in an improvement in the productivity, we "decrease" the h_0 to h_1 (or h_1 to h_2, etc.), where each larger subscript is understood to be an indefinitely *smaller* value.

$$h_0 \gg h_1 \gg h_2 \gg \ldots$$

3.2.6 – We will refer to each h_x as an *h-level*.

3.2.7 – We will call these values *partially-quantified* measures of productivity—as opposed to *fully-quantified* measures of productivity, given as normal fractions, e.g. $\frac{3}{7}$.

3.2.8 – This gives us a method of partially quantifying our productivity based on our present paradigm, without assuming any *absolute* scale of productivity, if needed.

3.2.9 – This may seem rather abstract—and it is—but we do put this algebra to use in §20.

3.2.10 – As an illustration, *any* number that is a fraction of h_1 is *greater than* any number that is a fraction of h_0, and so on.

$$Q(x) = \frac{100}{h_0}$$

$$Q(y) = \frac{1}{h_1}$$

$$Q(x) < Q(y)$$

3.2.11 – Or stated more precisely:

$$\forall x, y, n, m \left(\frac{x}{h_n} < \frac{y}{h_m} \right) : \left(x > 0 \land y > 0 \land n < m \right)$$

3.2.12 – When moving from one *h-level* to another, the productivity moves to a higher level than can be achieved on the previous level.

3.2.13 – For example, maybe we take pre-Galilean intuitions about mechanics to reside over h_0. Galileo's formulations raised the productivity of the descriptions incomparably to $\frac{1}{h_1}$. Over the intervening centuries and mechanics continued to evolved over h_1, say to $\frac{357}{h_1}$, then Newton raised the *h-level* of productivity to $\frac{1}{h_2}$ with his laws of motion and law of universal gravitation.

3.2.14 – Each *h-level* raises the level of productivity incomparably to the one previous.

3.2.15 – Productivity of a given *h-level* added to that of a higher *h-level* yields a value that is still meaningfully larger than the previous one:

$$\frac{x}{h_1} + \frac{y}{h_0} > \frac{x}{h_1}$$

3.2.16 – More precisely:

$$\forall x, y, n, m \left(\frac{x}{h_m} < \frac{x}{h_m} + \frac{y}{h_n} \right) : \left(x > 0 \wedge y > 0 \wedge n < m \right)$$

3.2.17 – The initial *h-level* h_0 is chosen arbitrarily; the remaining *h-levels* are chosen in relation to the initial *h-level* and to the other *h-levels*.

3.2.18 – We can also define multiplication of *h-values*. Take k to be a constant integer.

$$k\frac{x}{h_y} = \sum_{i=1}^{k} \frac{x}{h_y}$$

3.2.19 – The operation's behavior when multiplying *h-values* together is summarized below:

$$\forall x, y, n, m \left(\frac{x}{h_m} > \frac{x}{h_m} \cdot \frac{y}{h_n} \right) : \left(x > 0 \wedge y > 0 \right)$$

$$\forall w, x, y, z, n, m \left(w\frac{x}{h_m} > z\frac{y}{h_n} \right) : \left(x > 0 \wedge y > 0 \wedge w > 0 \wedge z > 0 \wedge m > n \right)$$

3.2.20 – A few examples to illustrate:

$$\frac{1}{h_0} \cdot \frac{1}{h_0} < \frac{1}{h_0} \cdot \frac{1}{h_1}$$

$$\frac{1}{h_0} \cdot \frac{1}{h_0} < \frac{1}{h_1} \cdot \frac{1}{h_1} \cdot \frac{1}{h_1} \cdot \frac{1}{h_1}$$

$$\frac{1}{h_0} < \frac{1}{h_1} \cdot \frac{1}{h_2} \cdot \frac{1}{h_3} \cdot \frac{1}{h_4} \cdot \ldots$$

$$\frac{1}{h_0} \cdot \frac{1}{h_{100}} < \frac{1}{h_1} \cdot \frac{1}{h_2} \cdot \frac{1}{h_3} \cdot \frac{1}{h_4} \cdot \ldots \cdot \frac{1}{h_{100}}$$

3.3 Non-Productivity & Counter-Productivity

3.3.1 – There is nothing to stop us from defining one specific helium atom in the Sun, one specific iron atom in the Earth's core, and one specific hydrogen atom in a distant star as "the Hydroplex." We could do this, but it would be entirely *non-productive* and the resulting concept would have no *domain*.

3.3.2 – We tend to use words that have some *productivity*—but not always. Language can be misused to create invalid concepts.

3.3.3 – For example, consider metaphysical entities like *justice*. If we ask "Does *justice* exist?" understood to mean something akin to "Does this table exist?" we have stretched our use of language to indicate a concept that cannot actually be instantiated in our minds.

3.3.4 – We must understand the context when we hear some such statement, that we ought to envision the question to ask, "Do events occur in the world which we would describe as *just?*"—not whether there is some separate entity in the world, called *justice*.

3.3.5 – We avoid this confusion this by ensuring that concepts we construct can actually be instantiated clearly in our minds.

3.3.6 – Some usage of language actively works against *productivity*. In these cases, we call the statement *counter-productive*.

3.3.7 – In *counter-productive* cases, we are led not only into confused or meaningless concepts, but are actively given the wrong answer to a question which has a right one.

3.3.8 – Imagine someone asks me, "What time is it?" I quickly look at my watch to see that it indicates 8:35. I then answer "9:15." In this example, I am giving an incorrect answer to a question which has a correct one. This is an example of *counter-productivity*.

3.3.9 – *Counter-productivity* can lead to negative values of productivity, e.g. $-\frac{1}{h_2}$.

3.3.10 – Productivity, along with *non-productivity* and *counter-productivity*, give us a measure for whether our concepts are useful or not. It begins to form the basis of the attribute we commonly call *truth*.

3.4 Measuring Productivity

3.4.1 – It is not possible in all circumstances, but *productive* use of language can be *fully-quantified* in some settings.

3.4.2 – Imagine an experiment with two people. Person A is given a five-dollar bill and two cups. Person A is instructed to hide the bill under one of the cups. When Person B enters the room, Person A is allowed only to say the words "right" or "left." The two people will split any money that is found successfully by Person B. Person B does not know what the game is or what the objective is.

3.4.3 – In the first trial, Person A hides the bill under the cup to his right-hand side. When Person B enters, Person A says "right." Person B looks under the cup to his own right and sees nothing. Person B leaves the room and the setup is tried again. Person B doesn't necessarily know that they failed at anything.

3.4.4 – In the second trial, Person A again hides the bill under the cup to his right. When Person B enters, he says "left" this time indicating Person B's left. Person B, though, suspects that there is an element of cooperation to the game and that they did not follow direction correctly. This time, Person B instead looks under the cup to Person A's right.

3.4.5 – This continues for a few rounds until both Person A and Person B settle on the same scheme—the instructions will be in relation to Person B's right and left. Where initially the chances of Person A and Person B getting the five-dollar bill are $\frac{1}{2}$ (50%), after a few iterations, they will soon have $\frac{1}{1}$ (100%) chance of getting the five-dollar bill each time the experiment is run.

3.4.6 – This is a clear quantitative demonstration of *fully-quantified productivity*.

3.4.7 – Not all instances of productivity are fully-quantifiable, but we've shown that productivity can be measured in some circumstances.

3.5 The Direction of Productivity

3.5.1 – We might ask, "Okay, so we can measure productivity sometimes. But how do we know that when they always get the five-dollar bill it's $\frac{1}{1}$, as in they get the bill 100% of the time—as opposed to $\frac{0}{1}$, as in they *don't* get the bill 0% of the time. Aren't we smuggling in a sense of one outcome being better than the other without any explanation for why we can do so?"

3.5.2 – We define getting the bill as more productive, because it is the more desired outcome *for those using the concepts*.

3.5.3 – Productivity is not a measure which has no subject in its scheme. Productivity is an attribute of *concepts*. Concepts require subjects.

3.5.4 – Our bias towards a certain outcome is justified *in the context of the subject using the concepts*.

4 Cognition

"This [guiding principle] may be termed the principle of the complete parallelism of the psychical and the physical. *According to our fundamental conception, which recognizes no gulf between the two provinces (the psychical and the physical), this principle is almost a matter of course."*

— Ernst Mach

The mind is most present to us, and yet often seemingly furthest from explanation. Let's take a closer look at what the mind *is*, and lay the groundwork for our more detailed investigations into how cognition operates in the chapters to come.

4.1 Correlates of the Mind

4.1.1 – The manifestations of the mind in the world are structures that match features of the mind's qualitative structure. That is, we expect the mind's other counterparts in the world to hold some properties that correspond to subjective properties of the mind.

4.1.2 – We will call these other counterparts of the world *correlates* of the mind.

4.1.3 – This isn't very hard to imagine. For example, a person on the north side of a mountain cannot see its south side. This is because the spatial locations of the mind's sensory input organs (i.e. its eyes) are not in a place that can gain sensory access to the south side of the mountain through visible light.

4.1.4 – The mind is not identical to its *correlates*; but it is not separable from them either. Cognition is a property of the relations between the mind's correlates.

4.1.5 – We need not say specifically what the natures of these correlates *are* (e.g. that they are neurons, or groups of neurons, or cerebral columns, or brain wave resonance patterns, or macromolecules, etc.) in order to describe *what we ought to look for* in finding them.

4.2 "Physical" & "Mental" Things

4.2.1 – We know that the world contains some arrangements of matter that correspond to conscious entities. But we *cannot* say that there are "physical" things that are separate from "mental" things.

4.2.2 – We can often get the sense that there are solid, tangible things in the world which are "physical" and other types of things which are "mental" that we experience.

4.2.3 – And there is no doubt that there are various manifestations of different kinds in the world. However, we know there is nothing solid or tangible about the "physical" things.

4.2.4 – At the most fundamental levels of our scientific description of the world, we only see equations and other mathematical structures that describe its behavior and structural relationships.

4.2.5 – But we don't know *what* the equations actually describe. This is a question of metaphysics that has largely been abandoned.

4.2.6 – We do not worry any longer about the *ontology* of the electron and all of its alien behaviors. We only care to describe them within a systematic framework.

4.2.7 – We will take the view that if you could describe systematically the patterns of relations that give rise to the mind, you will have at very least made great strides toward understanding the mind.

4.2.8 – We cannot insist on answers that concern the mind's "substance" any more than we can insist to know the "substance" of the electron.

4.2.9 – What we will do is to start from a basic description, and build on top of that a better description, and so on.

4.2.10 – The world contains electrons; the world contains minds. Instead of asking, *"What is the mind?"* we will ask the more productive questions: *"What does the mind do?"*, *"What relations are present within it?"*, and *"Can we describe them precisely?"*

4.2.11 – Once it was realized that the earth was round, the question *"Does it have an end?"* didn't make sense anymore. It may be that as the descriptions of the conscious mind are found, we will have a similar outcome.

4.3 Not *Just* a Computer

4.3.1 – The mind can perform computations. But it is not *just* a computer.

4.3.2 – Some of the mind's computations are conscious, as when you perform mental arithmetic.

4.3.3 – But the most complex computations the mind performs are not conscious.

4.3.4 – A football wide receiver tracking a ball through the air is performing a number of complex computations, simultaneously and constantly error correcting for new input.

4.3.5 – Based on scanty data, his mind must estimate how far away the ball currently is, what its angle of trajectory is, where that places its expected point of contact with the ground, how far away that is, based on all of that, how long the ball will be in the air, and finally how fast and in which direction he must run to be in position to catch the ball.

4.3.6 – Though the method his mind uses to come to these conclusions is different from the equations of physics, the end result is—within some margin of error—the same.

4.3.7 – Countless other abilities we have in visual and auditory processing, our synthesis and parsing of language, and almost every other useful capability involve some computation.

4.3.8 – However, the phenomenal experience that each of us realizes subjectively *is not* a computation, in the same way that the light emitted from my computer screen is not a computation. The processes that determine what to show on the screen *are* computational. But the backlit screen itself and the colors that it emits are *not* computations.

4.3.9 – In the next chapter, we examine the structure of experience, the input to our minds through *perception*.

5 Perception

"Each of us believes himself to live directly within the world that surrounds him, to sense its objects and events precisely, and to live in real and current time. I assert that these are perceptual illusions... Each of us lives within the universe—the prison—of his own brain. Projecting from it are millions of fragile sensory nerve fibers, in groups uniquely adapted to sample the energetic states of the world around us: heat, light, force, and chemical composition. That is all we ever know of it directly; all else is logical inference."

— Vernon Benjamin Mountcastle

All concepts in the mind originate in our *experience*, and in the *perceptions* each experience is made of.

5.1 Perceptions

5.1.1 – Sensory data are the mind's primitives of input, but they are unavailable to the conceptual system directly.

5.1.2 – A perception is a specific sensation as made available to the conceptual system.

5.1.3 – For example, visual perceptions consist of color, motion, shape, pattern/texture, extension. Audio perceptions consist of tone, volume, pattern, duration.

5.1.4 – We also have emotional perceptions. We sense our own emotions in a manner similar to the sensation of a color or a sound. It occurs to us with limited ability for us to control it.

5.1.5 – A perception is an *aspect* of an experience. Each experience is presented to us as a set of perceptions.

5.1.6 – Each perception is unique to a particular state of the mind's *correlates*; by all indications the correlates are mostly or entirely within the brain.

5.1.7 – The quality of a perception corresponds to the relationships between its correlates.

5.2 Perceptual Structure

5.2.1 – Perceptions are not the same as sensations. We do not experience sensations directly, but only after they have been filtered and enhanced through our mind's conceptual structure.

5.2.2 – For example, when I look at a word, it is very hard for me to see only shapes—I see words first and must use effort to view the shapes as they are.

5.2.3 – My conceptual ability to read words has modified my basic visual perception system to include information beyond the basic arrangement of visual hues to include more structured and meaningful information.

5.2.4 – It is interesting that this can be done by a skill that is learned several years into life, as reading. Other truly expert skills can also be modified in this way, such as when a trained musician can hear and identify auditory tones.

5.2.5 – It likely also happens much more often early in development, with vastly more fundamental aspects of our perceptions.

5.2.6 – Our depth perception is clearly not innate to us in the same way as the two-dimensional array of electromagnetic input on our retinas are. Stereoscopic vision is a complex process that involves our minds contrasting the images we perceive from each eye separately, among many other tricks we have of discerning distance. And yet, our depth perception gives us close to the same perception of extension as left-right extension or top-bottom extension.

5.2.7 – Further, though our minds take in two separate images, it composes them into what we perceive as a single image.

5.2.8 – Our ability to visually discriminate objects is another example of the same capability to supplement the raw sensory data in order to give us a modified, richer perception.

5.2.9 – Clearly, our perceptions are not just as they are, even down to the identity of objects; these perceptions are laid on top of the raw sensory data.

5.2.10 – We do not see the world *as it is*—whatever that may mean—but instead we see a world that has been marked up and modified in ways that make our perception more useful to us.

5.3 Experience

5.3.1 – Perceptions are sensations as they presented to the conceptual system. They are indicated by lowercase Greek letters.

5.3.2 – An experience is the conjugation of our perceptions in a given state. Experience χ is identical to a set of perceptions $\{\alpha, ...\}$.

$$\chi \equiv \{\alpha, ...\}$$

5.3.3 – The mind tends to give the impression that each experience is a unity, a single thing unto itself. Yet we know that an experience is a structure made up of multiple perceptions.

5.3.4 – Our perceptions can be broken down further, and analyzed as a system of correlates—its *manifestation*.

5.4 Interpretation

5.4.1 – The operation I (*interpret*) takes a set of perceptions and translates them into a conceptual structure.

5.4.2 – The following shows the interpretation of a set of perceptions $\{\alpha, ...\}$ yielding conceptual structure a:

$$I(\{\alpha, ...\}) \to a$$

5.4.3 – The resulting conceptual structure a corresponds to a model of the source of those perceptions, the person's body and environment.

5.4.4 – Operation I yields different models, even given the same input, depending on the current state of the mind.

5.4.5 – This is most often represented with a set of perceptions denoted by an experience χ, in relation to the existing conceptual structures k:

$$I(\chi \mid k) \to a$$

6 Manifestation

"Almost all aspects of life are engineered at the molecular level, and without understanding molecules we can only have a very sketchy understanding of life itself."

— Francis Crick

With an outline of the conceptual-perceptual system at hand, we venture further to extend our descriptions to broader and deeper levels of representation.

6.1 Stratified Analysis

6.1.1 – In order to explain cognition, we cannot limit ourselves to one level of description.

6.1.2 – Instead we will begin at the conceptual level, introduced in §1 and §2, with the simple operations we've described that are available for us to discover through direct subjective experience.

6.1.3 – According to the properties found at the conceptual level, we will follow our analysis to describe specific relational properties of the mind at the level of manifested correlates of consciousness.

6.1.4 – We call this multi-layer approach that first describes cognitive processes, *as they are realized subjectively*, and works down through other levels of manifestation, *stratified analysis*.

6.2 Perceptual Manifestation

6.2.1 – We now define a *function M, manifest*, which takes a perception α and yields its set of its correlates. Note that M is not an operation in that it is *not* a process that occurs in time, but instead is a mapping indicates that α at the perceptual level is *equivalent to* its set of correlates $\{\mu_{\alpha_1}, \mu_{\alpha_2}, \dots, \mu_{\alpha_n}\}$.

$$M(\alpha) = \{\mu_{\alpha_1}, \mu_{\alpha_2}, \dots, \mu_{\alpha_n}\}$$

6.2.2 – The inverse of function M is K, *collect*, which takes a set of correlates $\{\mu_{\alpha_1}, \mu_{\alpha_2}, \dots, \mu_{\alpha_n}\}$ and yields their collected *concept*.

$$K(\{\mu_{\alpha_1}, \mu_{\alpha_2}, \dots, \mu_{\alpha_n}\}) = \alpha$$

6.2.3 – By definition, these functions are directly inverse.

$$M(K(\alpha)) \equiv K(M(\alpha)) \equiv \alpha$$

6.3 Conceptual Manifestation

6.3.1 – Similarly to perceptions, concepts also have a function M which takes a concept a and yields a set of correlates.

$$M(a) = \{\mu_{a_1}, \mu_{a_2}, \dots, \mu_{a_n}\}$$

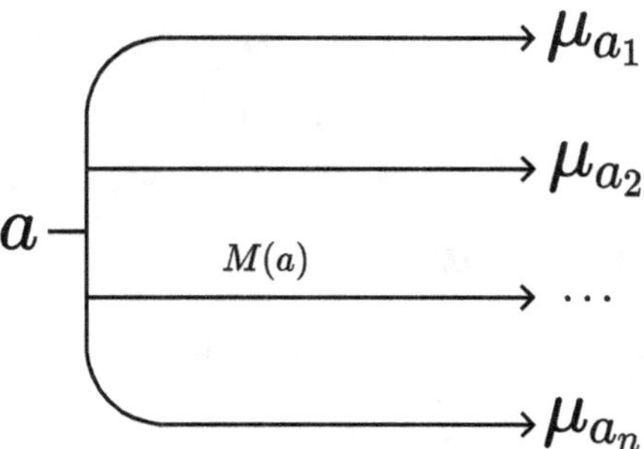

Figure 6: *Manifestation*: The concept a is manifested by its set of correlates $M(a) = \{\mu_{a_1}, \dots, \mu_{a_n}\}$.

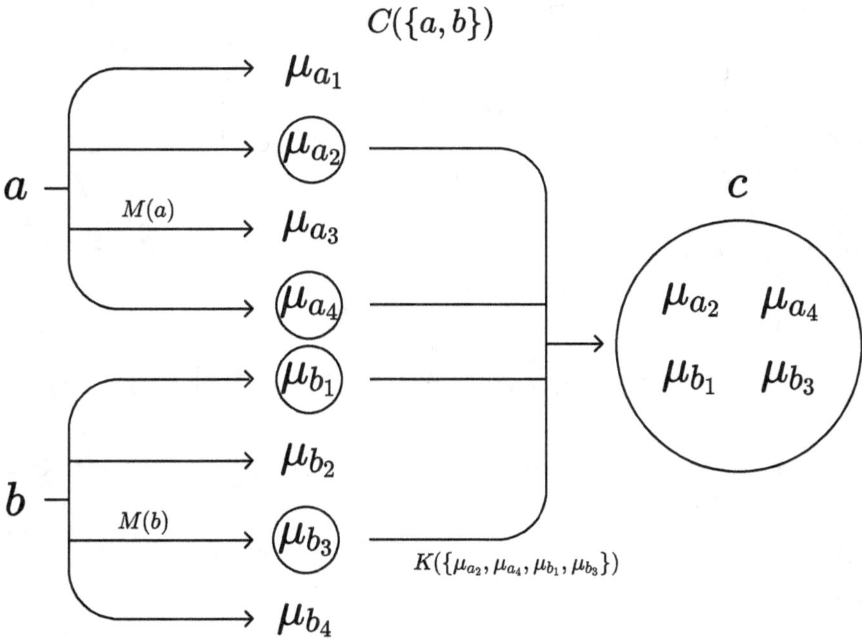

Figure 7: *Manifested Construction*: Construction combines subsets of the correlates from each of its components.

6.3.2 – Analogously, its inverse K:

$$K(\{\mu_{a_1}, \mu_{a_2}, \ldots, \mu_{a_n}\}) = a$$

$$M(K(a)) \equiv K(M(a)) \equiv a$$

6.4 Representation

6.4.1 – This method of describing manifestations is not only agnostic to the exact nature of the correlates within the world (i.e. neurons, cortical columns, etc.). But it is also flexible to more abstract descriptions laid on top of it.

6.4.2 – For example, we might be tempted to imagine each correlate represented by vertices in a graph or individual nodes in a sparse representation. However, it's important to keep in mind that the set of manifestations may just as well represent the *edges* in a graph or a specific *pattern* of sparse representation.

6.5 Construction

6.5.1 – We can now define the operation C at the level of manifestation. C takes a *subset* of the *correlates* of each of its components, and combines them via logical union into a new set of correlates, which new set *is* the constructed concept.

6.5.2 – Below S is a set of concepts with n members. A subset x_i of each concept S_i's correlates are combined via logical union into a set of correlates that are *collected* via function K into a newly constructed concept.

$$C(S) \equiv K\left(\bigcup_{i=1}^{n} x_i\right) : x_i \subseteq M(S_i) \wedge x_i \neq \{\}$$

6.5.3 – In other words, the constructed concept shares correlates with each of its components.

7 Conceptual Structure

"If the seemingly limitless multiplicity of color-sensations is susceptible to being reduced, by psychological analysis (self-observation), to six elements (fundamental sensations), a like simplification may be expected for the system of nerve-processes."

— Ernst Mach

A concept on its own serves hardly any use—except for the intricate web of relations it holds to other concepts, and the structures that are built between them.

7.1 Primitive Concepts

7.1.1 – Certain concepts cannot be *enumerated* further. They have no *components* except for themselves (though they may still have *relations*). We call these *primitive concepts*.

7.1.2 – We know subjectively that at least some of them are tied directly to our perceptions.

7.1.3 – These are concepts like «sound», «color», «anger», «pain», «time», «extension» (in space). Only direct experience of these things can properly account for them.

7.1.4 – Even a single experience of a perception can be abstracted and generalized from. But it cannot be done without the experience.

7.1.5 – We cannot describe these primitive concepts as general concepts through language alone, to someone who is not already familiar with them through their own experience. We cannot explain «red» to a person who was born blind.

7.1.6 – A blind person could have hallucinations of color, but they would never have any criteria for qualifying a specific color they hallucinated as one color or another, or even that what they experienced *was* a color.

7.1.7 – We *can* describe particular instances of primitive concepts in comparison to other instances of them. "As long as a football field." "Red-orange." "A honk like a train's horn." These make sense only in relation to other instances of the concept.

7.1.8 – When a primitive concept is *enumerated*, it yields only itself.

7.1.9 – The predicate Π indicates that its term is a primitive.

$$\Pi(j) \equiv E(j) \to j$$

7.1.10 – All other concepts can be *constructed* through specific associations of the primitive concepts.

7.2 Generalization

7.2.1 – Concepts are the echos of perceptions.

7.2.2 – Primitive concepts are not constructed, but are instead *generalized* from *perceptions* instead. Every primitive concept has been generalized from a perception or set of perceptions.

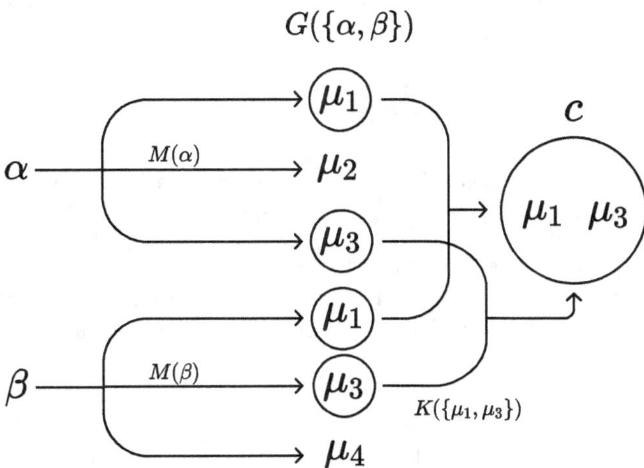

Figure 8: *Generalization*: Generalization creates a new concept by pooling common correlates from one or more perceptions. Pictured above, concept c is generalized from perceptions α and β.

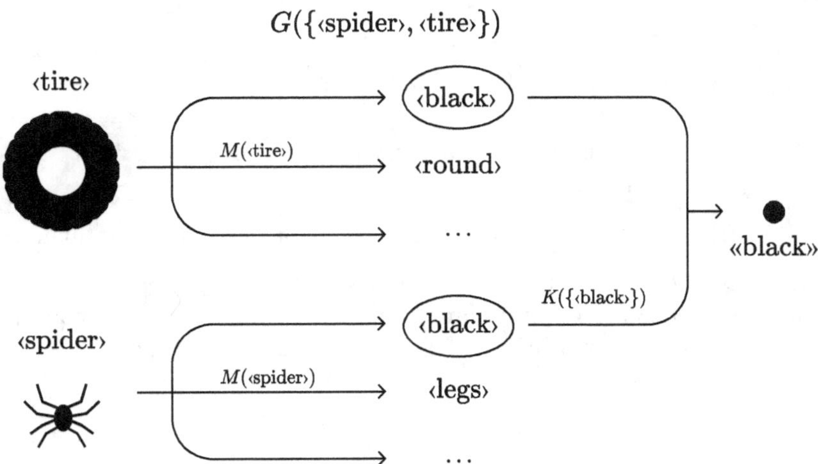

Figure 9: *Generalization Illustrated*: The concept «black» is *generalized* from the perceptions ⟨tire⟩ and ⟨spider⟩.

7.2.3 – We will take *generalization* to be an operation G which takes a set of one or more perceptions $\{\alpha, ...\}$ and generalizes from them a concept i, potentially a *primitive concept*.

$$G(\{\alpha, ...\}) \to i$$

7.2.4 – We will define G as the logical intersection of the manifestations of each of the perceptions it is generalized from.

7.2.5 – Below S is a set of perceptions with n members. A subset x_i of each perception S_i's correlates are combined via logical intersection into a set of correlates that are collected via function K into a newly constructed concept.

$$G(S) \equiv K\left(\bigcap_{i=1}^{n} x_i\right) : x_i \subseteq M(S_i), x_i \neq \{\}$$

7.2.6 – In other words, the constructed concept shares its correlates with *all* of its components—they are common to each member of S.

7.3 Conceptual Recursion

7.3.1 – Our minds can yield nearly infinite new concepts through the recursive combination of other concepts via the operation C.

$$C\Big(\{c\} \cup \big\{C(\{a,b\})\big\}\Big) \to d$$

7.3.2 – This is very similar to our capacity to produce practically infinite new English sentences.

7.3.3 – Although recursive, operation E does not have the same quality.

7.3.4 – Because of the existence of primitive concepts, all concepts can only be *enumerated* to some finite number of steps; once a primitive concept is obtained, repeated applications of E will yield the same concept.

$$E(a) \to b$$
$$E(b) \to c$$
$$...$$
$$E(y) \to z$$
$$E(z) \to z : \Pi(z)$$

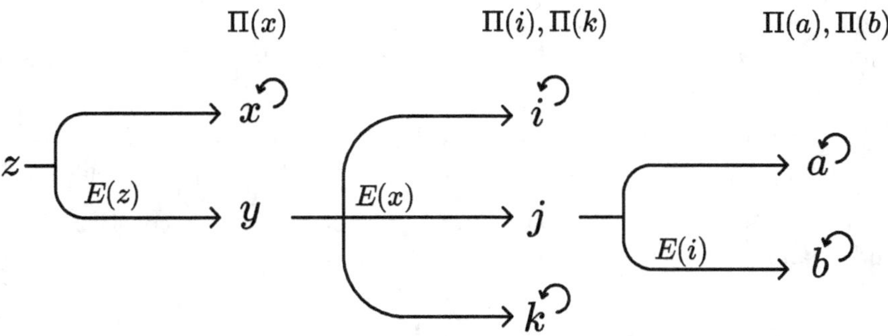

Figure 10: *Recursive Construction*: Concepts can be recursively *constructed* indefinitely.

Figure 11: *Recursive Enumeration*: Concepts can be recursively *enumerated* only until primitive concepts are encountered.

7.3.5 – This is for the same reason that all words in the dictionary will ultimately be found to be self-referential (directly or indirectly) or that one or more of the words in their definition will be directly or indirectly self-referential.

7.3.6 – Based on our reasoning here, we are making a potentially testable empirical claim. We are saying that our minds *must generalize* primitive concepts from perceptions before other *complex* concepts can be constructed.

7.4 Relationships

7.4.1 – Each subsequent mental state is a modification of the previous one; it is not replaced all at once.

7.4.2 – When perceptions lead to correlates that are shared by existing concepts, those concepts will tend to result from each other.

7.4.3 – We can now give a more explicit account of when two concepts are related: namely, that two concepts, perceptions, or other mental entities are related *if they share common correlates.*

$$\Phi(a,b) \equiv \Big(M(a) \cap M(b) \neq \{\} \Big)$$

7.4.4 – This can happen explicitly, as between a concept and its components.

$$\Big(C(\{a\}) \to b \Big) \Rightarrow \Big(M(a) \cap M(b) \neq \{\} \Big) \Rightarrow \Phi(a,b)$$

7.4.5 – It may also occur implicitly. For example, perception α always or usually co-occurs with perception β.

7.4.6 – In such circumstances, when concept c is *generalized* from α, some correlates of β may be included in the correlates of c, causing a relation.

7.4.7 – Let's consider the example of two experiences: χ_0 consisting of α and β, and χ_1 consisting of only β.

$$\chi_0 = \{\alpha, \beta\}, \ \chi_1 = \{\beta\}$$
$$\Big(G(\chi_0) \to c \Big) \Rightarrow \Big((M(c) \cap M(\alpha) \neq \{\}) \wedge (M(c) \cap M(\beta) \neq \{\}) \Big)$$
$$G(\chi_1) \to d$$

7.4.8 – When $M(c) \cap M(\beta) \cap M(d) \neq \{\}$:

$$\Phi(c,d)$$

7.4.9 – Relations between concepts indicate that when the mind is in the state represented by one concept, there is some probability that it will lead causally to the other concept.

7.4.10 – In other words, $\Phi(a, b)$ means that when the mind is in the state indicated by concept a, there is some probability that it will be followed by the state indicated by concept b.

7.4.11 – We indicate this probability as $\Phi^*(b \mid a)$, the probability that b will result from state a:

$$\Phi^*(b \mid a) \in [0, 1]$$

7.4.12 – The sum of all Φ^* following from a is equal to 1:

$$\forall a \sum_{x \in R(a)} \Phi^*(x \mid a) = 1$$

7.4.13 – We can also state these probabilities in terms of a sequence of multiple states leading to them. For example, $\Phi^*(c \mid b \mid a)$ represents the probability that c will follow b after b follows a.

7.4.14 – And similar to the above from §7.4.12:

$$\forall a \sum_{x \in R(a)} \sum_{y \in R(x)} \Phi^*(y \mid x \mid a) = 1$$

7.4.15 – Because these values are probabilities, all of a concept's relations—in terms of probability—tend to weaken as more relationships are added.

8 Semantic Operations

"Meaning is what essence becomes when it is divorced from the object of reference and wedded to the word."

— W.V.O. Quine

In order to cover the breadth of our experience, a significant piece is missing: the ability to specify the semantic nature of the relationships between conceptual structures.

8.1 Conceptual Relationships

8.1.1 – Now given the operations we have defined, we can specify relationships between concepts and conceptual structures, but we are not able to specify what the nature of those relationships are.

8.1.2 – Let's take as example the sentence *Bob kicks the ball*. We could imagine a simple structure defined in terms of C to represent it:

$$C(\{\text{«Bob», «kick», «the ball»}\}) \rightarrow \text{«Bob kicks the ball»}$$

8.1.3 – This would combine each of the component concepts «Bob», «kick», and «the ball», as we've set out to. But a problem arises: how can we distinguish *what is being kicked* from *what is doing the kicking*.

8.1.4 – To specify this semantic relationship, we define a new type of concept called a *component class*.

8.2 Component Classes

8.2.1 – A *component class* serves as a template for some other concept which can be substituted for it.

8.2.2 – From our above example, the concept «kick» has two roles implied within it: the [kicker]—i.e. *the thing doing the kicking*—and the [kickee]—i.e. *the thing being kicked*. We will specify component classes as terms inside square brackets.

8.2.3 – Further, each component class can have its own structure. For example:

$$C(\{\text{«has a foot», «can apply force»}\}) \rightarrow \text{«kicker»}$$

8.2.4 – And also:

$$C(\{\text{«physical object»}\}) \rightarrow \text{«kickee»}$$

8.2.5 – These statements mean that a «kicker» must have the components represented by «has a foot» and «can apply force», and that a «kickee» must have the component represented by «physical object», respectively.

8.2.6 – Note that in this context, they are referred to as «kicker» and «kickee», as opposed to [kicker] and [kickee].

8.2.7 – The reason is because «kicker» and «kickee» are just normal concepts like any other. It's only in the context of «kick» that they are *parameters*,

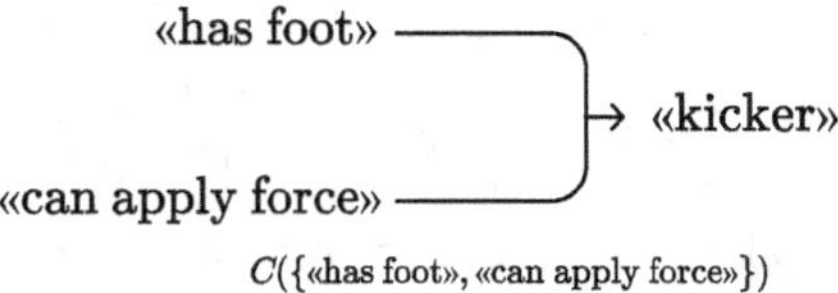

Figure 12: *Kicker Definition*: Definition of «kicker». When combined with the proxy, «kicker» becomes the component class [kicker].

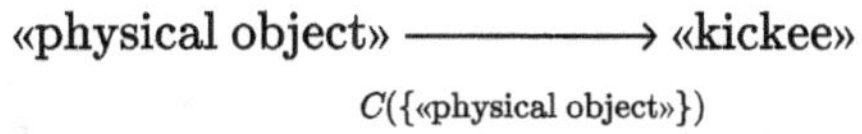

«physical object» ⟶ «kickee»

$C(\{\text{«physical object»}\})$

Figure 13: *Kickee Definition*: Definition of «kickee». When combined with the proxy, «kicker» becomes the component class [kickee].

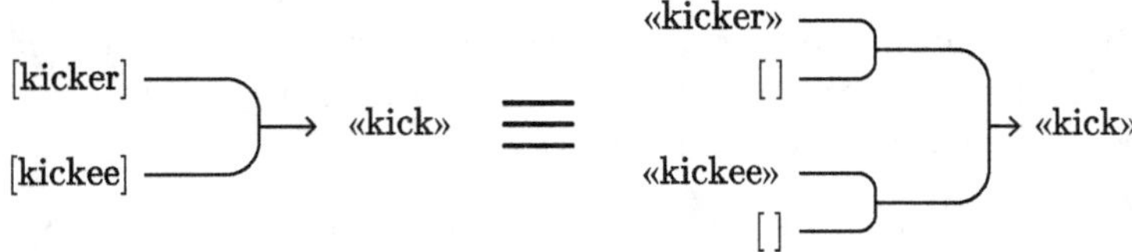

Figure 14: *Kick Definition*: Definition of «kick», shown with the shorthand for component classes and its equivalent conceptual structure.

meaning that they serve as a placeholder or template for some other concept that can be substituted. In that context, we say that «kick» has been *parameterized*.

8.2.8 – When a concept is *tagged* into a *component class* we represent that by using operation C to construct the component class, which we call the *tag*, with the symbol [ ], which we refer to as the *proxy*.

8.2.9 – A component class is the construction of a concept with the *proxy*. Shown by example:

$$C(\{\text{«kicker»}, [\,]\}) \to [\text{kickee}]$$

8.3 Construction Shorthand

8.3.1 – Because the structures we build are becoming more complex, let's introduce a new shorthand for C to improve legibility:

$$C(\{a, b\}) \equiv \langle a, b \rangle$$

8.3.2 – For example, the definition of «kick» from above can be written as:

$$\text{«kick»} = \Big\langle \langle \text{«kicker»}, [\,] \rangle, \langle \text{«kickee»}, [\,] \rangle \Big\rangle$$

8.3.3 – Or equivalently:

$$\text{«kick»} = \Big\langle [\text{kicker}], [\text{kickee}] \Big\rangle$$

8.4 Class Matching

8.4.1 – In order to put *component classes* to use, our minds need a method for determining whether one concept matches the structure of the one that serves as the *tag* for the component class.

8.4.2 – Let's define a new predicate Υ, which indicates that concept a *matches* the *tag* b.

8.4.3 – However first, we need a predicate to determine whether a concept itself is *parameterized*, which we will denote Υ'. Υ' is part of Υ, and is defined here separately for legibility only.

$$\Upsilon'(a) \equiv \forall x \exists y (x \in E(a) \wedge y \in E(x) \wedge y = [\,])$$

8.4.4 – Now, the definition of Υ:

$$\Upsilon(a, r) \equiv \forall x \in E(r) \begin{cases} |E(a)| > 0 & \text{if } x = [\,] \\ [\,] \in E(a) & \text{if } x = [\cdot] \\ \forall y \in E(a)\,\Upsilon(y, x) & \text{if } \Upsilon'(x) \\ x \in E(a) & \text{otherwise} \end{cases}$$

8.4.5 – If $\Upsilon(a, r)$, we say that *a matches r*.

8.4.6 – Stated differently, every component of b is also a component of a, except for $[\,]$, which matches any concept, and $[\cdot]$, which matches exactly $[\,]$.

8.4.7 – $[\cdot]$, the *dot proxy*, is a new symbol that allows us to match the *proxy symbol itself*, instead of using it as a placeholder.

8.4.8 – We denote the version of any concept that has its $[\,]$s replaced with $[\cdot]$ by placing a dot over it, as below:

$$[\dot{\text{kicker}}] = \langle \text{«kicker»}, [\cdot] \rangle$$

8.4.9 – Shown by example, the following produce matches:

$$\Upsilon(a, a)$$

$$\Upsilon([\,], [\cdot])$$

$$\Upsilon\Big(\langle \text{«has a foot»}, \text{«can apply force»}, \dots \rangle, \text{«kicker»}\Big)$$

$$\Upsilon\Big(\langle \text{«kicker»}, \text{«Fred»} \rangle, \langle \text{«kicker»}, [\,] \rangle\Big)$$

$$\Upsilon\Big(\langle \langle \text{«kicker»}, \text{«Joe»} \rangle, \langle \text{«kickee»}, [\,] \rangle \rangle, \text{«kick»}\Big)$$

8.4.10 – And the following do not:

$$\neg\Upsilon\Big(\langle \text{«has a foot»} \rangle, \text{«kicker»}\Big)$$

$$\neg\Upsilon\Big(\text{«some other concept»}, \text{«kickee»}\Big)$$

$$\neg\Upsilon(\text{«not-proxy»}, [\cdot])$$

8.4.11 – A *matched* concept transitively shares *all* of its *relations* with the concepts it *matches*:

$$\Upsilon(a,b) \Rightarrow \forall x \Big(x \in R(b) \Rightarrow x \in R(a) \Big)$$

$$\forall x \Big(x \in R(b) \Rightarrow x \in R(a) \Big) \Rightarrow \forall x \Big(\Phi(b,x) \Rightarrow \Phi(a,x) \Big)$$

8.4.12 – In addition to the predicate Υ, we also define an operation Y, *match*, which yields «true» when its first argument matches the second argument, and «false» otherwise:

$$Y(a,r) \equiv \begin{cases} \text{«true»} & \text{if } \Upsilon(a,r) \\ \text{«false»} & \text{otherwise} \end{cases}$$

8.5 Transclusion

8.5.1 – The ability to match conceptual structures based on patterns is potentially useful for building new structures with a semantic context.

8.5.2 – But we can only put this capability to use if we can substitute conceptual structures into others.

8.5.3 – We need a method of replacing a component class with a concrete concept.

8.5.4 – Operation T, *transclude*, substitutes b for the concept tagged r in a:[5]

$$T(a,r,b) \to a' : \Upsilon(b,r)$$

$$T(a,r,b) \equiv C\Big((E(a) \setminus \{\langle r,[\,]\rangle\}) \cup \{\langle r,b\rangle\} \Big)$$

8.5.5 – When b is substitutes for r's *proxy* through *transclusion*, it leaves the tag in place to indicate its class:

$$\text{«kick»} = \Big\langle [\text{kicker}], [\text{kickee}] \Big\rangle = \Big\langle \langle \text{«kicker»},[\,]\rangle,\ [\text{kickee}] \Big\rangle$$

$$\text{«Bob»} = \Big\langle \text{«has foot»}, \text{«can apply force»}, \ldots \Big\rangle$$

$$T(\text{«kick»}, \text{«kicker»}, \text{«Bob»}) \to \text{«kick»}'$$

$$: \text{«kick»}' = \Big\langle \langle \text{«kicker»}, \text{«Bob»}\rangle,\ [\text{kickee}] \Big\rangle$$

8.5.6 – We can then apply transclusion again to transclude «the ball» as the [kickee].

---

[5]The proper definition of T replaces $\langle r,[\,]\rangle$ with $X(a,r)$, defined in the next section, so that the substitution generalizes to any concept tagged r.

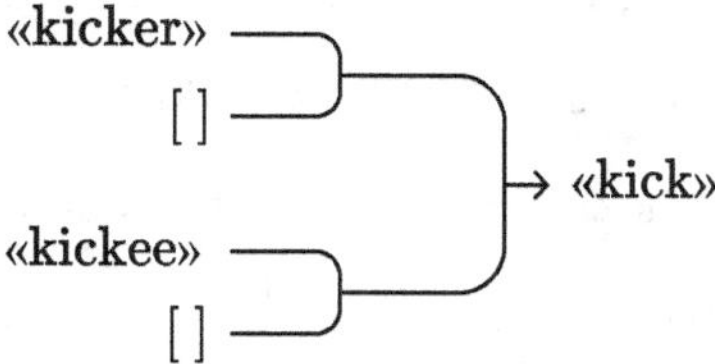

Figure 15: *Kick Definition*: Recall our definition of «kick».

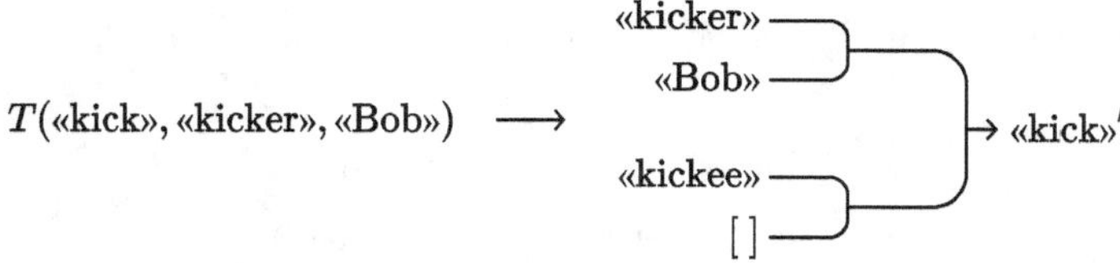

Figure 16: *Transclusion Illustration 1*: Transclusion from «kick» to «kick»′. «Bob» is trancluded for [kicker].

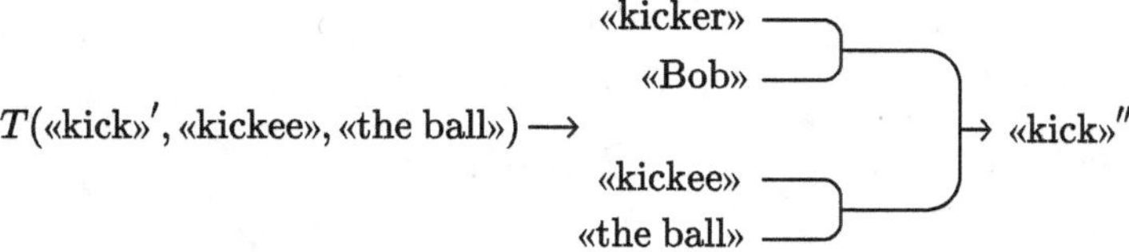

Figure 17: *Transclusion Illustration 2*: Transclusion from «kick»′ to «kick»″. «the ball» is trancluded for [kickee].

$$\text{«the ball»} = \Big\langle \text{«physical object»}, \dots \Big\rangle$$

$$T(\text{«kick»}', \text{«kickee»}, \text{«the ball»}) \to \text{«kick»}''$$

$$: \text{«kick»}'' = \Big\langle \langle \text{«kicker»}, \text{«Bob»}\rangle, \ \langle \text{«kickee»}, \text{«the ball»}\rangle \Big\rangle$$

$$: \text{«kick»}'' = \text{«Bob kicks the ball»}$$

8.6 Extraction

8.6.1 – Now that we can transclude concepts into other concepts, fulfilling its semantic roles, we need an operation where we can *extract* a transcluded concept from another.

8.6.2 – Below $X(a', r)$ extracts the concept *tagged* with r from a' to yield b:

$$X(a', r) \to b$$

8.6.3 – From our example above:

$$X(\text{«kick»}'', \text{«kicker»}) \to \text{«Bob»}$$
$$X(\text{«kick»}'', \text{«kickee»}) \to \text{«the ball»}$$

8.6.4 – When there is no such concept, the *null concept* $\emptyset$ is yielded:

$$X(\text{«kick»}'', \text{«some concept»}) \to \emptyset$$

8.6.5 – One thing to note is that X doesn't necessarily have to operate on a concept that was produced via T. Any concept can *tag* another if they have been composed.

$$C\Big(\big\{ C(\{a, b\}), \ c \big\}\Big) \to d$$
$$X(d, b) \to a$$
$$X(d, a) \to b$$

8.6.6 – In other words X is defined in terms of structure, as opposed to how the structure was obtained.

8.6.7 – Because of its common use, we will often denote X by an alternate syntax for legibility:

$$X(a, \text{«concept»}) \equiv a[\text{concept}]$$

8.7 Manifested Definitions

8.7.1 – Predicate $\Upsilon(a, r)$ indicates that every manifestation of r is also a manifestation of its *match* a:

$$\Upsilon(a, r) \equiv \forall x(x \in M(r) \Rightarrow x \in M(a))$$

8.7.2 – Recall from §7.4.3:

$$\Phi(a, b) \equiv \Big(M(a) \cap M(b) \neq \{\} \Big)$$

8.7.3 – We can now prove the theorem that every *matched* concept *must* share relations with its match:

$$x \in M(r) \Rightarrow \Big(x \in M(r) \wedge x \in M(a) \Big)$$

$$\Big(x \in M(r) \wedge x \in M(a) \Big) \Rightarrow \Big(M(r) \cap M(a) \neq \{\} \Big)$$

$$\therefore \forall y \Big(\Phi(r, y) \wedge \Upsilon(a, r) \Big) \Rightarrow \Phi(a, y)$$

8.7.4 – Operation T removes from the manifestation of a, the complement of the manifestation of r and another set r'—where the manifestation of r' is a subset of the manifestation of a and a superset of the manifestation of r— and replaces the removed set with the manifestation of b. r' is understood to be the composition of r and $[\,]$.

8.7.5 – More formally:

$$T(a, r, b) \rightarrow a'$$

$$: a' \equiv K\Big(\Big(M(a) \setminus (M(r') \setminus M(r)) \Big) \cup M(b) \Big)$$

$$: \exists r' \Big(M(r) \subset M(r') \subseteq M(a) \wedge M(r) \subseteq M(b) \Big)$$

8.7.6 – Operation X is defined using a similar structure in reverse.

8.7.7 – Operation X yields a subset from the manifestation of a', the manifestation r''—where the manifestation of r'' is a subset of the manifestation of a' and a superset of the manifestation of r.

$$X(a', r) \rightarrow b$$

$$: b \equiv K\Big(M(r'') \Big)$$

$$: \exists r'' \Big(M(r) \subset M(r'') \subseteq M(a') \Big)$$

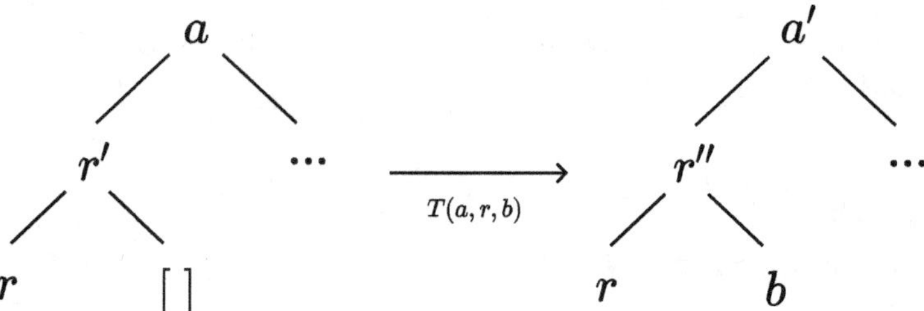

Figure 18: *Transclusion*: An illustration of $T(a, r, b) \to a'$ depicting the operation structurally.

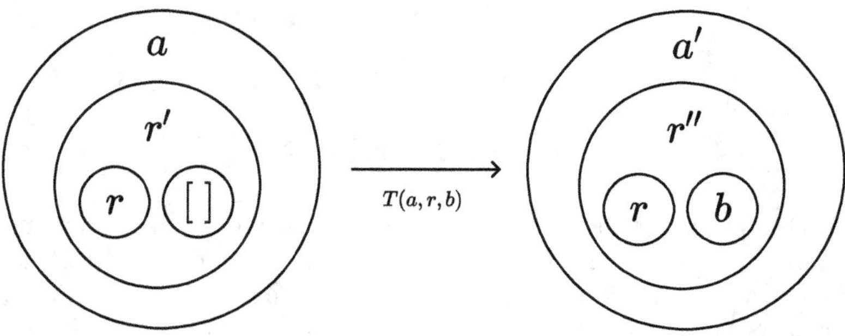

Figure 19: *Manifested Transclusion*: In this diagram, the concentric circles and symbols represent subsets of a's manifestations. The operation substitutes the manifestation of the proxy for the manifestation of b.

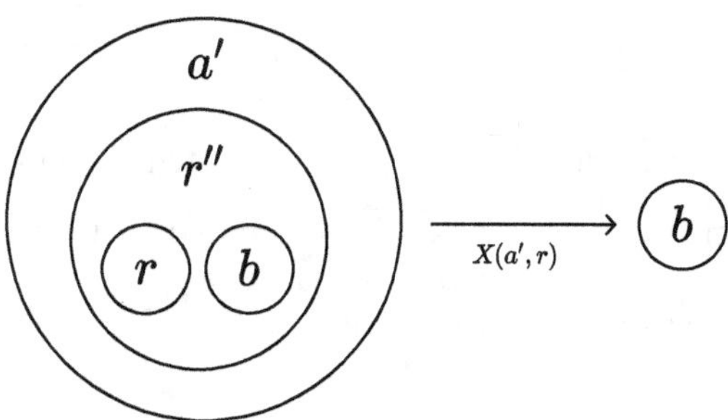

Figure 20: *Manifested Extraction*: This diagram shows the extraction of the concept b tagged by r from a', denoted $X(a', r) \to b$.

9 Mechanical Framework

"We do not know what the rules of the game are; all we are allowed to do is to watch the playing. Of course, if we watch long enough, we may eventually catch on to a few of the rules."

— Richard Feynman

We now have a full account of the fundamental operations within the system. In this chapter we will restate them to give us a clear picture of our framework.

Moving forward, we show that limiting ourselves only to simple operations we have defined so far, we can create and manipulate a vast array of new conceptual structures and mechanisms.

9.1 Basic Operations

9.1.1 – Operation *C*, *compose*, enables us to construct new concepts from existing ones. This capability is an essential property of the human mind.

> E.g. *I combine my concepts* «tall» *and* «tree» *into a* «tall tree».

9.1.2 – Operation *E*, *enumerate*, gives us a method for recalling the components of a concept in a hierarchical manner; it will only yield direct components of its argument.

> E.g. *A* «dead grass» *is a composition of my concepts* «dead» *and* «grass».

9.1.3 – When operation *C* is applied, it creates *relations* between its arguments. The relations are the propensity for the mind in the state of one concept to subsequently lead to a state consisting of another concept.

> E.g. «big city» *holds relations to* «big», «city», «Chicago», *and other concepts.*

9.1.4 – Operation *R*, *recount*, is the operation that enacts this change of state from one concept to one or more of its related concepts.

> E.g. *The concept* «city» *may remind me of* «big city». «big city» *may remind me of* «Chicago». «Chicago» *may remind me of* «trains».

9.1.5 – Operation *R* also gives us a way to establish connections between concepts in a non-hierarchical way, as opposed to the inherently hierarchical, structure-preserving nature of operation *E*.

> E.g. *The concept* «city» *may remind me of* «trains», *without thinking of* «Chicago» *or any other concept between.*

9.2 Perceptual Operations

9.2.1 – Operation *I*, *interpret*, takes a perception as an argument and produces an analogous concept.

> E.g. *When I see a* ‹rectangle›, *the instantiation of a* «shape» *takes place in my mind.*

9.2.2 – Operation G takes a set of perceptions as its argument, and yields a new concept from their common correlates.

> E.g. $G(\{\langle\text{wool}\rangle, \langle\text{cotton}\rangle, \langle\text{dandelion}\rangle\})$ *may generalize the visual texture* «fuzzy».

9.3 Semantic Operations

9.3.1 – Operation T, *transclude*, enables us to substitute conceptual structures into other conceptual structures in a way that enforces semantic limitations. T is the ability to create concrete structures from abstract ones.

> E.g. *The concept* «drive» *has component classes for* [driver] *and* [vehicle]. *I can transclude* «John» *into* «drive» *as the* [driver], *and* «my truck» *as the* [vehicle], *to yield the new concept* «John driving my truck».

9.3.2 – Operation X, *extract*, gives us the ability to obtain conceptual structures contained within others based on semantic and structural criteria.

> E.g. *From* «John driving my truck», *I can extract the* «driver»— «John»—*and the* «vehicle»—«my truck».

9.3.3 – Operation Y determines whether one conceptual structure *matches* that of another.

> E.g. «John» *matches* «driver», *but not* «my truck».

9.4 Manifestations

9.4.1 – Mapping M gives the representation of a mental entity at the level of the correlates.

> E.g. $M(\text{«}John\text{»})$ *may represent some pattern of neuronal activity in the brain.*

9.4.2 – Mapping K inversely takes a representation at the correlate level, and yields a mental entity.

> E.g. $K(\{\mu_1, \mu_2, \mu_3\})$ *may manifest the concept* «shovel».

10 Memory

"We learn by rearranging what we know."

— Ludwig Wittgenstein

No system of cognition can serve much purpose without a system for storing and accessing the mental entities available to it. In the chapter that follows, we begin to show how memory materializes itself within our framework.

10.1 Memory

10.1.1 – Memory is the ability to replicate aspects of a previous mental state (i.e. to recall concepts).

10.1.2 – Memory has two essential aspects. There must be some *representation*, that is stored; and there must be some *mode of access* to restore the state within the representation.

10.1.3 – To have some stored representation is useless if it can't be accessed again at a later time.

10.2 Associative Learning

10.2.1 – Associative learning is the development of the mechanisms that store *representations* and their *modes of access* to function more productively.

10.2.2 – Operation L, *learn*, then is defined as a new operation that takes a, combines it with the already existing concept b to construct a':

$$L(a \mid b) \to a' \equiv C(\{a, b\}) \to a'$$

$$: M(a') = A \cup B : A \subseteq M(a), B \subseteq M(b)$$

10.2.3 – From implication of the above, we can prove the theorem that a and b are now related such that when b is *recounted* a is a possible result:

$$L(a \mid b) \Rightarrow \Big(\Phi(a', a) \wedge \Phi(b, a') \Big)$$

$$\Phi(b, a') \Rightarrow \Big(R(b) \to \{a', ...\} \Big)$$

$$\Phi(a', a) \Rightarrow \Big(R(a') \to \{a, ...\} \Big)$$

$$\therefore R(b) \to \{a, ...\}$$

10.2.4 – In the description above, $M(a')$ is the *representation* of a, and $R(b)$ is the *mode of access* to a'.

10.2.5 – The probability that recounting b will produce a is given as follows:

$$\Phi^*(a \mid b) = \Phi^*(a' \mid b) \cdot \Phi^*(a \mid a')$$

10.2.6 – This is a demonstration of associative learning, where one concept becomes related to another such that the concept of one can produce another by being *recounted*.

10.2.7 – This operation can be expanded so that the *learned* concept a becomes associated with more than one other concept, represented by the set of concepts S:

$$L(a \mid S) \to a' \equiv C(\{a\} \cup S) \to a'$$

$$L(a \mid S) \Rightarrow \Phi'(\{a'\} \cup S) \wedge \Phi(a', a)$$

$$\therefore R(x) \to \{a, ...\} : x \in S$$

10.2.8 – With the probability of this occurence given as:

$$\Phi^*(a \mid x) = \Phi^*(a' \mid x) \cdot \Phi^*(a \mid a')$$

10.2.9 – Or in the case that every member of S should be included:

$$\Phi^*(a \mid S) = \sum_{s \in S} \Phi^*(a' \mid s) \cdot \Phi^*(a \mid a')$$

11 Numbers & Quantity

In the following chapter, we observe how simple mathematical structures cleanly fall out of the conceptual framework we have developed, almost entirely without modification.

11.1 Varieties of Quantity

11.1.1 – While we often think of them as the same, the mind has many conceptual models of numbers and quantities.

11.1.2 – The simplest concept of quantity is centered only around the ideas "more," "less," "the same"—or stated alternatively "a lot," "a little," "somewhere in between." We will call this capability *estimation*.

11.1.3 – The next simplest numeric capability is that of discrete pattern recognition. This is the ability to pick out a number of items purely based on a visual pattern.

11.1.4 – For example, you can look at a set of four balls, and determine purely based on pattern alone that there are indeed *four* balls—without counting or any other iterative process. This capability is called *subitization*.[6]

11.1.5 – The average human capability for subitization usually hits its limit at four to five items.[7]

11.1.6 – Some animals, including chimpanzees and parrots, have been shown to be capable of subitization.[8]

11.1.7 – Beyond subitization, humans are also capable of *counting*, the recursive enumeration of quantities. Only human beings are known to be able to count.

11.1.8 – Humans are, of course, capable of even further representations of numbers and quantity—including digital numbers, complex numbers, etc.—via intentional construction of new conceptual paradigms.

11.1.9 – In the following sections, we will explore conceptual representations of two of these paradigms: *counting* and *digital numbers*.

11.1.10 – The representations that follow are meant as plausible conceptual representations of these numerical types. However, it is almost certain that each person has slightly different conceptual instantiations of each, and even may have slightly different instantiations at different times, or multiple alternative structures she may choose from.

11.1.11 – We will restrict ourselves only to using the fundamental operations that have already been defined previously. This leaves a solid foothold for the idea that our numerical ability is a spandrel—an evolutionary side effect—of our conceptual capabilities outlined previously.

---

[6]Tomonaga & Matsuzawa (2002).
[7]Ibid.
[8]See Tomonaga & Matsuzawa (2002) and Pepperberg (1994).

11.2 Counting & Successor

11.2.1 – In order to represent counting numbers, we will need a conceptual representation of zero, and an operation to obtain the next counting number.[9]

11.2.2 – Our representation of zero will be composed of the concept «num», which will serve as a tag, and the proxy:

$$\text{«}0_c\text{»} \equiv \langle \text{«num»}, [\ ] \rangle$$

11.2.3 – The c subscript indicates that it is a *counting* number.

11.2.4 – Let's define the *successor* operation H_0, the operation that yields the next counting number after the number given:[10]

$$H_0(n) \equiv \langle \text{«num»}, n \rangle$$

11.2.5 – Note that is equivalent to the following definition in terms of C:

$$H_0(n) \equiv C(\{\text{«num»}, n\})$$

11.2.6 – To illustrate:

$$\text{«}1_c\text{»} \equiv H_0(\text{«}0_c\text{»}) \equiv \Big\langle \text{«num»}, \langle \text{«num»}, [\ ] \rangle \Big\rangle$$

$$\text{«}2_c\text{»} \equiv H_0(\text{«}1_c\text{»}) \equiv \Big\langle \text{«num»}, \big\langle \text{«num»}, \langle \text{«num»}, [\ ] \rangle \big\rangle \Big\rangle$$

11.2.7 – And so on. From here forward, we will use the notation «n_c» to denote the concept of the counting number n.

11.2.8 – Note that although we may denote the number with two digits, e.g. «17_c», there is no concept within the counting numbers of multiple digits. The only significance of «17_c» is that it is the counting number after «16_c», which is the counting number after «15_c», etc.

---

[9]This idea is borrowed from a field called *Peano arithmetic*, named for the Italian mathematician, Giuseppe Peano.

[10]Also from *Peano arithmetic*, *successor* is the conventional term which produces the next natural number after a given one. H_0 represents the zeroth *hyperoperation*. Hyperoperations are successive arithmentical operations, starting from the successor, through addition, multiplication, exponentiation, tetration (repeated exponentiation), etc.

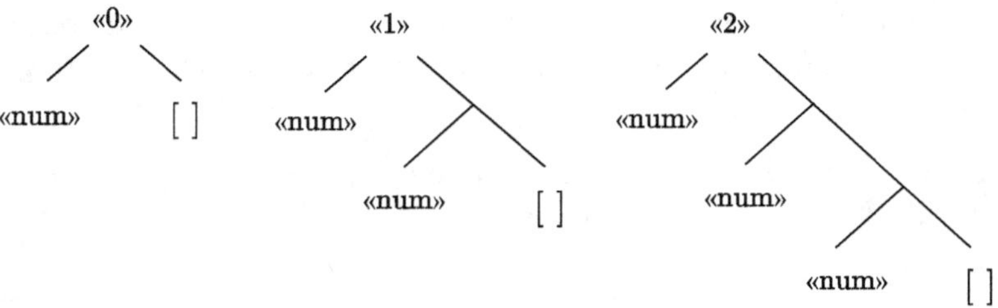

Figure 21: *Counting Numbers*: This graphic shows the conceptual structures «0», «1», and «2».

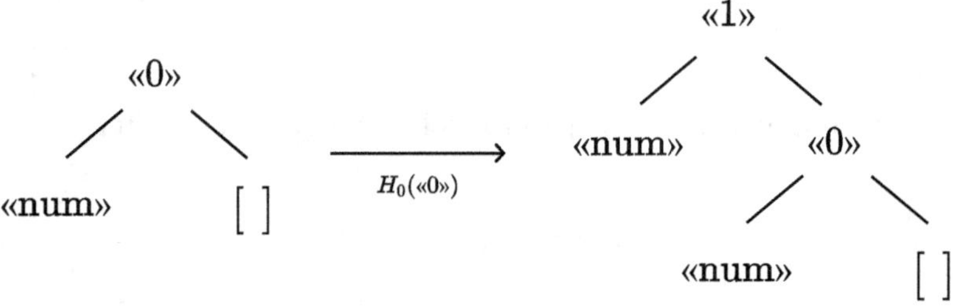

Figure 22: *Successor*: The successor operation H_0 is depicted above to yield «1» from «0» by composing «0» with «num».

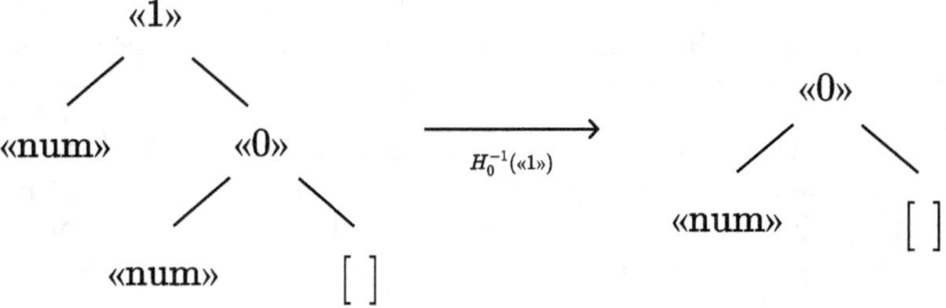

Figure 23: *Anti-Successor*: The anti-successor operation H_0^{-1} is depicted above to yield «0» from «1» by extracting the «0» tagged with «num».

11.3 Anti-Successor

11.3.1 – We may also define the inverse of H_0, the *anti-successor* H_0^{-1}, which takes a counting number and yields the number previous:

$$H_0^{-1}(n) \equiv X(\langle n \rangle, \text{«num»})$$

11.3.2 – By example:

$$H_0^{-1}(\text{«}1_c\text{»}) \equiv X\Big(\big\langle \langle \text{«num»}, \langle \text{«num»}, [\,] \rangle \rangle \big\rangle, \text{«num»}\Big)$$

$$H_0^{-1}(\text{«}1_c\text{»}) \to \langle \text{«num»}, [\,] \rangle$$

11.3.3 – From §11.2.2 above, $\langle \text{«num»}, [\,] \rangle$ is the definition of «0_c», thus:

$$H_0^{-1}(\text{«}1_c\text{»}) \to \text{«}0_c\text{»}$$

11.3.4 – From here forward, for notational convenience, unless otherwise specified, any concept given simply as «n» will be understood to be «n_c».

$$\text{«}0\text{»} \equiv \text{«}0_c\text{»}$$

$$\text{«}532\text{»} \equiv \text{«}532_c\text{»}$$

11.4 Comparison

11.4.1 – We'll need a way to compare these newly defined quantities.

11.4.2 – We will say that one counting number a is greater than or equal counting number b *if a and b are numerals and a matches b.*

11.4.3 – Notice that:

$$\Upsilon\Big(\big\langle \text{«num»}, \langle \text{«num»}, [\,] \rangle \big\rangle, \big\langle \text{«num»}, [\,] \big\rangle \Big)$$

11.4.4 – And, of course:

$$\Upsilon\Big(\big\langle \text{«num»}, [\,] \big\rangle, \big\langle \text{«num»}, [\,] \big\rangle \Big)$$

11.4.5 – But not:

$$\neg\Upsilon\Big(\big\langle \text{«num»}, [\,] \big\rangle, \big\langle \text{«num»}, \langle \text{«num»}, [\,] \rangle \big\rangle \Big)$$

11.4.6 – We notice also that all counting numbers match «0», so for clarity we define «any-num», such that for any counting number n, $\Upsilon(n, \text{«any-num»})$:

$$\text{«any-num»} \equiv \text{«0»}$$

11.5 Sequences

11.5.1 – We can also use our existing operations to define simple sequences.

11.5.2 – Each element of the sequence will be given a numeric key, corresponding to the index of its order within the sequence.

11.5.3 – Since we will use numerals to indicate both the index and value of each member of the sequence, we introduce a new specifier κ.

11.5.4 – κ composes the provided concept with a concept «key», to distinguish it from the numerical value of the equivalent numeral:

$$\kappa(n) \equiv C(\{n, \text{«key»}\})$$

11.5.5 – As a shorthand, we will indicate these *keyed* concepts with an overbar:

$$\kappa(n) \equiv \bar{n}$$

$$\kappa(\text{«53»}) \equiv \text{«}\overline{53}\text{»}$$

11.5.6 – In order to preserve consistency with the remainder of our operations, we also define the following identities for basic counting operations:

$$H_0(a) \to b \iff H_0(\bar{a}) \to \bar{b}$$

$$H_0^{-1}(a) \to b \iff H_0^{-1}(\bar{a}) \to \bar{b}$$

11.5.7 – For example:

$$H_0(\text{«0»}) \to \text{«1»} \implies H_0(\text{«}\bar{0}\text{»}) \to \text{«}\bar{1}\text{»}$$

$$H_0^{-1}(\text{«4»}) \to \text{«3»} \implies H_0^{-1}(\text{«}\bar{4}\text{»}) \to \text{«}\bar{3}\text{»}$$

11.5.8 – Below we have our empty sequence, «sequence»:

$$\text{«sequence»} \equiv \langle \rangle$$

11.5.9 – We can now write to our empty «sequence» via T:

$$T(\text{«sequence»}, \text{«}\bar{0}\text{»}, n) \to i$$

$$: i = \Big\langle \langle \text{«}\bar{0}\text{»}, n \rangle \Big\rangle$$

$$T(i, \text{«}\bar{1}\text{»}, m) \to j$$

$$: j = \Big\langle \langle \text{«}\bar{0}\text{»}), n \rangle, \langle \text{«}\bar{1}\text{»}, m \rangle \Big\rangle$$

11.5.10 – Note that T in this usage does not enforce the structural requirements that it does when used to transclude concepts with semantic content. Transcluding a *key* ignores the semantic requirements.

11.5.11 – We can then later retrieve the values with X', an analog of X which returns «0» instead of $\emptyset$ when the given key doesn't exist.

11.5.12 – X' will yield the «sequence»'s value at the given key in the sequence, if it exists; otherwise it will yield «0»:

$$X'(a,r) \equiv \begin{cases} \text{«0»} & \text{if } X(a,r) = \emptyset \\ X(a,r) & \text{otherwise} \end{cases}$$

11.5.13 – We will give a definition X' in terms of fundamental operations as a conceptual machine in §12.4.1.

11.5.14 – Continuing the example above:

$$X'(j, \text{«}\bar{0}\text{»}) \to n$$

$$X'(j, \text{«}\bar{1}\text{»}) \to m$$

11.5.15 – When the given key doesn't yet exist in the sequence we yield the default value «0»:

$$X'(j, \text{«}\bar{31}\text{»}) \to \text{«0»}$$

11.5.16 – In practice, we will usually omit the X' notation; in any case where X is applied to a «sequence», it is understood to be an application of X', including in the shorthand notation.

$$j[\bar{31}] \to \text{«0»}$$

12 Conceptual Machines

In this chapter we set the simple elements of our framework to use building *conceptual machines*, automata that enact our mathematical and computational abilities.

12.1 The Structure of a Conceptual Machine

12.1.1 – A conceptual machine consists of a set of conceptual structures and their relations. The conceptual structures determine template states for the conceptual structures that a machine acts upon.

12.1.2 – Each state's relations determine transformation rules for the following state from each template.

12.1.3 – According to the theorem developed in §8.7.3, every concept that matches the structure of the state transitively shares the state's relations.

12.1.4 – Each relation performs transformations on the template concept by use of existing operations, or their combinations. All transformations ultimately reduce either directly to a fundamental operation, or a combination of fundamental operations.

12.1.5 – This allows us to create patterns of behavior that are embodied in the machines. We can define transformations on families of matched concepts instead of specific concrete concepts. We will see these at work in the following sections.

12.2 A Composing Machine

12.2.1 – In order to demonstrate conceptual machines, we will develop a simple composing machine, $\mathcal{M}_C$ which will take two concepts and produce a composition of them via operation C.

12.2.2 – To define the potential *states* of the machine, we will first need a *state specifier*. A specifier is a template for a conceptual structure, and an associated notation to make its meaning more clear.

12.2.3 – *State specifiers* are denoted σ.

12.2.4 – In the present case of our composing machine, we define σ_C:

$$\sigma_c(s, c_1, c_2) \equiv \Big\langle \langle \text{«state»}, s \rangle, \langle \text{«op1»}, o_1 \rangle, \langle \text{«op2»}, o_2 \rangle \Big\rangle$$

12.2.5 – With the tag «state» and its possible values:

$$\Upsilon(\{\text{«begin»}, \text{«end»}\}, \ \text{«state»})$$

12.2.6 – This is a new shorthand that stands for:

$$\Upsilon(\text{«begin»}, \text{«state»}) \wedge \Upsilon(\text{«end»}, \text{«state»})$$

12.2.7 – The «begin» state indicates that the operation has not yet applied. «end» indicates that the operation has been applied, and prevents further application of the same operation.

12.2.8 – «op1» and «op2» represent arbitrary conceptual structures with no structural requirements. «op1» and «op2» are the inputs to C, and «op2» becomes the product of the operation after it is applied.

12.2.9 – Below, we define a machine state which represents the machine before the operation has been applied, an indication to the machine that there is work to be done.

12.2.10 – First, s_{0_C}, the state before the operation is applied:

$$s_{0_C} = \sigma_C(\text{«begin»}, \ [\ ], \ [\ ])$$

12.2.11 – Notice that the structure this produces matches a structure with *any* concept for «op1» and «op2».

12.2.12 – With our state defined, we now need to define a relation. In this case, instead of using our Φ notation, we're going to use a new notation that invokes operation R directly. This notation makes it more clear that we are defining a transformation.[11]

$$R(s_{0_C}) \rightarrow \sigma_C(\text{«end»}, \ [\ ], \ \langle s_{0_C}[\text{op1}], s_{0_C}[\text{op2}]\rangle)$$

12.2.13 – Stated in plain language, what the above says is *when recounting a concept that matches the structure of s_{0_C}*, replace its «state» with «end», replace its «op1» with the proxy, and replace its «op2» with the composition of its «op1» and «op2».

12.2.14 – Notice that we only denote one product of the operation, as opposed to a set of products as in its definition in §2.4.12. This is allowed by the rule of operations §2.1.16, and it implies that $\Phi^*(s_{0_C}, R(s_{0_C})) = 1$, i.e. that no other resultant states are possible.

12.2.15 – Certainly, we know in an actual mind no mechanism is perfect; it is far to complex for such black and white measures. But in our context, we do want a deterministic transformation, wherein each time the conceptual machine is in a certain state, exactly one state is the correct subsequent state.

12.2.16 – We could imagine machines that are not deterministic and are instead stochastic.[12] These types of machines clearly offer rich possibilities for future exploration, but they are not covered in this work.

---

[11]Note the use of the alternate syntax for operation X, defined in §8.6.7.

[12]These machines could be modeled as Markov processes.

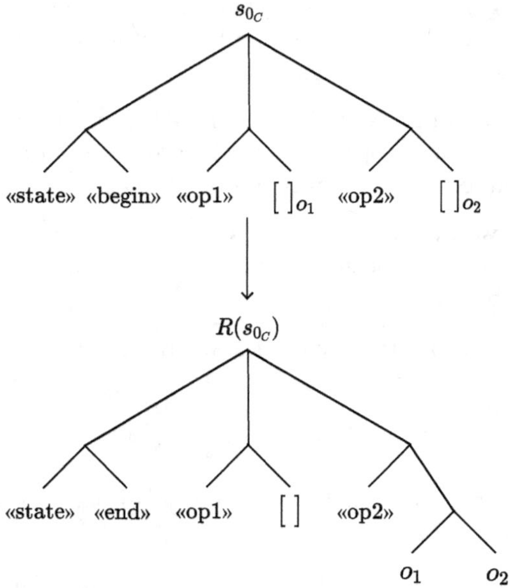

Figure 24: *Composing Machine Structure*: Here we see a general representation of the state s_{0_C} and its transformation via $R(s_{0_C})$.

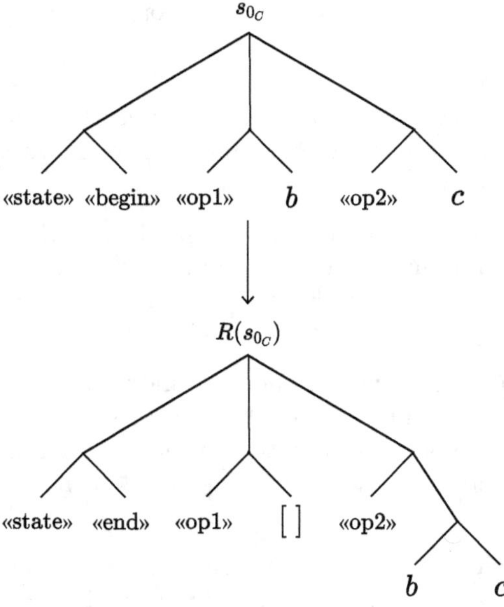

Figure 25: *Composing Machine Evaluated*: This illustrates a concrete enactment of the transformation rule indicated above.

12.2.17 – In this case we need only one defined state for our entire machine. Once the transformation from the first state has occurred, no further work is required.

12.2.18 – Let's introduce the definition of the machine itself, which is simply the set of its of states. We denote machines as $\mathcal{M}$, with a subscript to denote which specific machine it is.

$$\mathcal{M}_C = \{s_{0_C}\}$$

12.2.19 – In order to make the workings of our machine $\mathcal{M}_C$ more obvious, let's give a couple concrete examples:

$$s_{ex_1} = \sigma_C(\text{«begin»},\ b, c)$$

$$R(s_{ex_1}) \to \sigma_C(\text{«end»},\ [\,],\ \langle b, c \rangle)$$

$$s_{ex_2} = \sigma_C(\text{«begin»},\ \text{«comfy»},\ \text{«couch»})$$

$$R(s_{ex_2}) \to \sigma_C(\text{«end»},\ [\,],\ \langle \text{«comfy»}, \text{«couch»} \rangle)$$

12.3 Machine Specifiers

12.3.1 – We now introduce a new type of specifier, which we will call *machine specifiers*. Machines specifiers simply define the initial state of the machine as an alias of a state specifier.

12.3.2 – The first machine specifier we will define for $\mathcal{M}_C$ will set the «state» to «begin» and will accept arguments for the other parameters to σ_C.

$$\mathcal{M}_C(o_1, o_2) \equiv \sigma_C(\text{«begin»},\ o_1,\ o_2)$$

12.3.3 – To illustrate its function:

$$\mathcal{M}_C(\text{«fast»}, \text{«car»}) \equiv \sigma_C(\text{«begin»},\ \text{«fast»},\ \text{«car»})$$

12.3.4 – We can also specify an alternate version that takes only one argument and allows us to set an initial default state for «op2»:

$$\mathcal{M}_C(o_1) \equiv \sigma_b(\text{«iter»},\ o_1,\ \text{«some-default-value»})$$

12.4 X' Machine

12.4.1 – Let's give a definition of X' from §11.5.12 now fully in terms of fundamental operations as a conceptual machine.

12.4.2 – First, our machine specifier $\sigma_{X'}$:

$$\sigma_{X'}(s,t,v,r) \equiv \Big\langle \langle \text{«sequence»}, s\rangle, \langle \text{«tag»}, t\rangle, \langle \text{«value»}, v\rangle, \langle \text{«result»}, r\rangle \Big\rangle$$

12.4.3 – The first state moves «sequence»'s value of «tag» into «value»:

$$s_{0_{X'}} = \sigma_{X'}([\,], [\,], [\cdot], [\cdot])$$

$$R(s_{0_{X'}}) \to \sigma_{X'}\Big(s_{0_{X'}}[\text{sequence}], \ s_{0_{X'}}[\text{tag}],$$
$$X(s_{0_{X'}}[\text{sequence}], s_{0_{X'}}[\text{tag}]), \ [\,] \Big)$$

12.4.4 – Our second state sets «result» to «0» when «value» is $\emptyset$, and cleans up the remainder of the structure:

$$s_{1_{X'}} = \sigma_{X'}([\,], [\,], \emptyset, [\cdot])$$

$$R(s_{1_{X'}}) \to \sigma_{X'}([\,], [\,], [\,], \text{«0»})$$

12.4.5 – If «value» *is* set, our third state moves «value» into «result» and cleans up the remainder of the structure.

$$s_{2_{X'}} = \sigma_{X'}([\,], [\,], [\,], [\cdot])$$

$$R(s_{2_{X'}}) \to \sigma_{X'}([\,], [\,], [\,], s_{2_{X'}}[\text{value}])$$

12.4.6 – Notice that the order here matters. We take the order of the state definitions to be the order they are matched in. If $s_{2_{X'}}$ were defined before $s_{1_{X'}}$, the default state would never be reached.

12.4.7 – Now we can define our machine specifier $\mathcal{M}_{X'}$ for operation X' in terms of its state specifier $\sigma_{X'}$, and a restated definition of operation X':

$$\mathcal{M}_{X'}(s,t) \equiv \sigma_{X'}(s,t,[\,],[\,])$$

$$X'(a,r) \equiv X\Big(R(\mathcal{M}_{X'}(a,r)), \text{«result»} \Big)$$

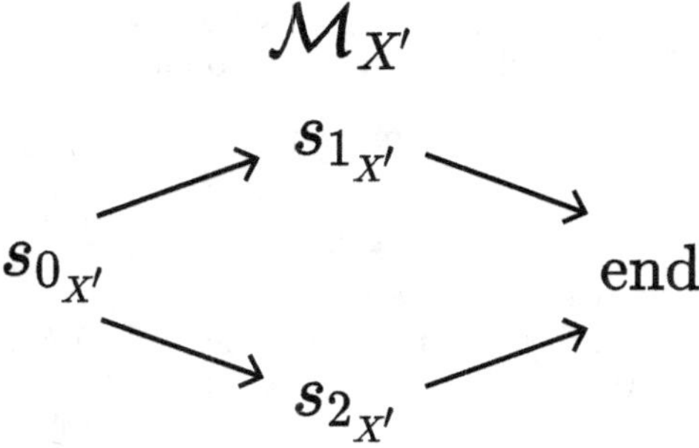

Figure 26: *X′ State Graph*: This graph shows the possible state transitions of $\mathcal{M}_{X'}$. Note the branching between $s_{1_{X'}}$ and $s_{2_{X'}}$, depending on whether «sequence»'s value of «tag» is set.

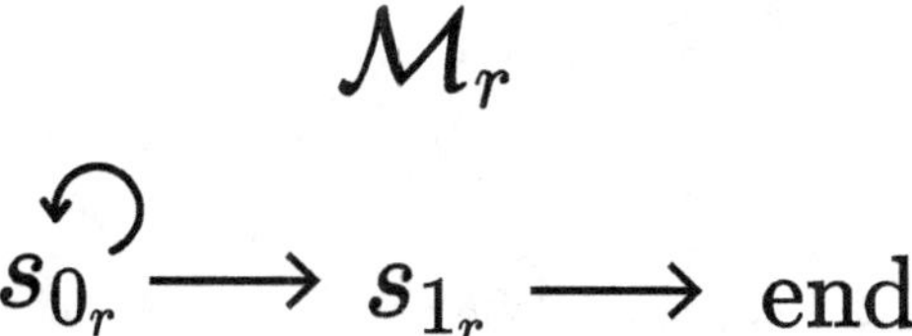

Figure 27: *Repeating Machine State Graph*: The repeating machine $\mathcal{M}_r$ iterates in its initial state s_{0_r} until it completes.

12.5 A Repeating Machine

12.5.1 – It's often necessary in any number of mental operations to repeat a task some set number of times. We will see an illustration of this in practice below.

12.5.2 – Let's define a new machine $\mathcal{M}_r$ which repeats an operation according to the number of times supplied by a given counting number.

12.5.3 – In plain English, our machine will:

1. Perform R on a given structure s.
2. Decrement a numeric counter n.
3. Substitute given values for particular tagged components in s.
4. If $n \neq$ «0», repeat from #1; otherwise stop.

12.5.4 – First let's define the machine's conceptual structure:

$$\sigma_r(s, n, t, v) \equiv \Big\langle \langle \text{«structure»}, s \rangle, \langle \text{«num»}, n \rangle, \langle \text{«tag»}, t \rangle, \langle \text{«value»}, v \rangle \Big\rangle$$

12.5.5 – This machine takes a conceptual «structure» s, likely defined by some other specifier, a «num» of times to complete the operation n, a «tag» t which indicates a component of s which will be overwritten after each operation, and a «value» v, which will be overwritten to the component tagged by t.

12.5.6 – The «tag» and «value» allow us to reset the state of the structure, so that it resumes a form that can be evaluated again by R.

12.5.7 – Let's first define s_{0_r}, the state when there are still n times yet to complete the operations, where $n \neq$ «0»:

$$s_{0_r} = \sigma_r([\,], \text{«not-0»}, [\,], [\,])$$

12.5.8 – Here we take «not-0» as equivalent to «1», because every number other than «0» matches «1» via $\Upsilon(x, \text{«1»})$.

$$\text{«not-0»} \equiv \text{«1»}$$

12.5.9 – We then apply the operation we are repeating, which is the same as applying operation R to structure $s_{0_r}[\text{structure}]$:

$$R(s_{0_r}[\text{structure}]) \to s_{0_r}[\text{structure}]'$$

12.5.10 – s_{0_r} of our repeating machine yields the next state through the following relation:

$$R(s_{0_r}) \to \sigma_r\Big(T(s_{0_r}[\text{structure}]', s_{0_r}[\text{tag}], s_{0_r}[\text{value}]),$$
$$H_0^{-1}(s_{0_r}[\text{num}]),\ s_{0_r}[\text{tag}],\ s_{0_r}[\text{value}]\Big)$$

12.5.11 – The repeating machine concludes when $n = \text{«0»}$:

$$s_{1_r} = \sigma_r([\,], \text{«}\dot{0}\text{»}, [\,], [\,])$$
$$R(s_{1_r}) \to \sigma_r(s_{1_r}[\text{structure}], [\,], [\,], [\,])$$

12.5.12 – For legibility, we often show our states in an *instruction table*:

	s	$R(s)$
s_{0_r}		
«structure»	[ ]	$T(s_{0_r}[\text{structure}]', s_{0_r}[\text{tag}], s_{0_r}[\text{value}])$
«num»	«not-0»	$H_0^{-1}(s_{0_r}[\text{num}])$
«tag»	[ ]	$s_{0_r}[\text{tag}]$
«value»	[ ]	$s_{0_r}[\text{value}]$
s_{1_r}		
«structure»	[ ]	$s_{1_r}[\text{structure}]$
«num»	«$\dot{0}$»	[ ]
«tag»	[ ]	[ ]
«value»	[ ]	[ ]

12.5.13 – We may need to reset more than one value after each repetition. In practice, we will use σ_r with an arbitrary number of replacements:

$$\sigma_r(s, n, t_1, v_1, t_2, v_2, ...) \equiv$$
$$\Big\langle \langle\text{«structure»}, s\rangle, \langle\text{«num»}, n\rangle, \langle\text{«tag-1»}, t_1\rangle, \langle\text{«value-1»}, v_1\rangle,$$
$$\langle\text{«tag-2»}, t_2\rangle, \langle\text{«value-2»}, v_2\rangle, ... \Big\rangle$$

12.5.14 – We will skip showing the definition for each version of σ_r for brevity. They will follow the following pattern:

$$\mathcal{M}_r(s, n) \equiv \sigma_r(s, n, [\,]\ldots)$$

$$\mathcal{M}_r(s, n, t, v) \equiv \sigma_r(s, n, t, v, [\,]\ldots)$$

$$\mathcal{M}_r(s, n, t_1, v_1, t_2, v_2) \equiv \sigma_r(s, n, t_1, v_1, t_2, v_2, [\,]\ldots)$$

$$\ldots$$

12.6 Compound Machines

12.6.1 – In some cases, we may want to combine the behavior of one or more other machines. We call these combinations of machines *compound machines.*

12.6.2 – There are two ways to combine the behavior of machines. The first is structurally, wherein we use a specifier from one machine to specify part of another machine. The other is relationally, in which the behavior of one machine is included inside another via its usage in defining a relation or relations between states.

12.6.3 – We are going to illustrate both methods in machines that display equivalent behavior below. Both machines repeatedly apply operation C using $\mathcal{M}_C$. One of them achieves this structurally using the machine specifiers of $\mathcal{M}_C$ and $\mathcal{M}_r$ (i.e. §12.7) and another does so relationally by invoking $R(\mathcal{M}_C)$ inside the definition of another machine's relations (i.e. §12.8).

12.7 Structurally Compound Machines

12.7.1 – For our structural compound example, let's combine the specification of $\mathcal{M}_C$ and $\mathcal{M}_r$ into a new machine structure.

$$s_{ex_3} = \mathcal{M}_r(\mathcal{M}_C(\text{«A»}, \text{«B»}),\ \text{«3»},\ \text{«state»},\ \text{«begin»},\ \text{«op1»},\ \text{«A»})$$

12.7.2 – The above is equivalent to the more explicit structure:

$$s_{ex_3} = \Big\langle \langle \text{«structure»},\ \mathcal{M}_C(\text{«A»}, \text{«B»})\rangle \langle \text{«num»}, \text{«3»}\rangle,$$

$$\langle \text{«tag1»}, \text{«state»}\rangle, \langle \text{«value1»}, \text{«begin»}\rangle, \langle \text{«tag2»}, \text{«op1»}\rangle, \langle \text{«value2»}, \text{«A»}\rangle \Big\rangle$$

12.7.3 – Where $\mathcal{M}_C(\text{«A»}, \text{«B»})$ is, from above:

$$\mathcal{M}_C(\text{«A»}, \text{«B»}) =$$

$$\Big\langle \langle \text{«state»}, \text{«begin»}\rangle, \langle \text{«op1»}, \text{«A»}\rangle, \langle \text{«op2»}, \text{«B»}\rangle \Big\rangle$$

12.7.4 – This operation ought to compose «A» into the «op2» 3 times, yielding a new structure that is 3 levels deep.

12.7.5 – Let's see it in action:

	«structure»	«num»
$R(s_{0_r}) \rightarrow s_{0_r}$	$\mathcal{M}_C(«\text{A}», «\text{B}»)$	«3»
	$\mathcal{M}_C([\,], \langle «\text{A}», «\text{B}» \rangle)$	«3»
$R(s_{0_r}) \rightarrow s_{0_r}$	$\mathcal{M}_C(«\text{A}», \langle «\text{A}», «\text{B}» \rangle)$	«2»
	$\mathcal{M}_C([\,], \langle «\text{A}», \langle «\text{A}», «\text{B}» \rangle \rangle)$	«2»
$R(s_{0_r}) \rightarrow s_{1_r}$	$\mathcal{M}_C(«\text{A}», \langle «\text{A}», \langle «\text{A}», «\text{B}» \rangle \rangle)$	«1»
	$\mathcal{M}_C([\,], \langle «\text{A}», \langle «\text{A}», \langle «\text{A}», «\text{B}» \rangle \rangle \rangle)$	«1»
$R(s_{1_r})$	$\mathcal{M}_C([\,], \langle «\text{A}», \langle «\text{A}», \langle «\text{A}», «\text{B}» \rangle \rangle \rangle)$	«0»

12.8 Relationally Compound Machines

12.8.1 – Now let's look at an equivalent relationally compound machine. This method requires we that define a new machine that utilizes another machine (or machines) within its relations.

12.8.2 – Our machine will produce the same result, $\langle «\text{A}», \langle «\text{A}», \langle «\text{A}», «\text{B}» \rangle \rangle \rangle$, through another methodology.

12.8.3 – This machine will operate on the same principles as the repeating machine, but in actual practice relationally compound machines can give more flexibility than would be gained from the structurally compound machine above.[13]

12.8.4 – First we will define an operation in terms of $\mathcal{M}_C$:

$$C_{op}(o_1, o_2) \equiv X(R(\mathcal{M}_C(o_1, o_2)), «\text{op2}»)$$

12.8.5 – Then we define a simple machine to repeat the operation:

$$\sigma_{rc}(o_1, o_2, n) = \Big\langle \langle o_1, «\text{op1}» \rangle, \ \langle o_2, «\text{op2}» \rangle, \ \langle n, «\text{num}» \rangle \Big\rangle$$

---

[13]In the latter chapters of the book we will see that any machine, including compound relational machines, can be represented structurally; but we will ignore this caveat for the time being.

12.8.6 – Our first defined state matches when there are remaining repetitions represented by n. Note the usage of C_{op}.

$$s_{0_{rc}} = \sigma_{rc}([\,], [\,], \text{«not-0»})$$

$$R(s_{0_{rc}}) \rightarrow \sigma_{rc}(s_{0_{rc}}[\text{op1}],\ C_{op}(s_{0_{rc}}[\text{op1}], s_{0_{rc}}[\text{op2}]),\ H_0^{-1}(s_{0_{rc}}[\text{num}]))$$

12.8.7 – And our second state defines the completed state after the repeated C_{op} has been applied, with the result in «op2»:

$$s_{1_{rc}} = \sigma_{rc}([\,], [\,], \text{«}\dot{0}\text{»})$$

$$R(s_{1_{rc}}) \rightarrow \sigma_{rc}([\,],\ s_{1_{rc}}[\text{op2}], [\,])$$

12.8.8 – Let's illustrate with an analogous example to §12.7:

$$s_{ex_4} = \sigma_{rc}(\text{«A»}, \text{«B»}, \text{«3»})$$

$$R(s_{ex_4}) \rightarrow \sigma_{rc}([\,], \langle \text{«A»}, \langle \text{«A»}, \langle \text{«A»}, \text{«B»} \rangle \rangle \rangle, [\,])$$

12.8.9 – Step-by-step below:

	«op1»	«op2»	«num»
$R(s_{0_{rc}}) \rightarrow s_{0_{rc}}$	«A»	«B»	«3»
$R(s_{0_{rc}}) \rightarrow s_{0_{rc}}$	«A»	$\langle \text{«A»}, \text{«B»} \rangle$	«2»
$R(s_{0_{rc}}) \rightarrow s_{0_{rc}}$	«A»	$\langle \text{«A»}, \langle \text{«A»}, \text{«B»} \rangle \rangle$	«1»
$R(s_{0_{rc}}) \rightarrow s_{1_{rc}}$	«A»	$\langle \text{«A»}, \langle \text{«A»}, \langle \text{«A»}, \text{«B»} \rangle \rangle \rangle$	«0»
$R(s_{1_{rc}})$	[ ]	$\langle \text{«A»}, \langle \text{«A»}, \langle \text{«A»}, \text{«B»} \rangle \rangle \rangle$	[ ]

13 Arithmetical Machines

"When we talk mathematics, we may be discussing a secondary language, built on the primary language truly used by the central nervous system."

— John von Neumann

In this chapter, we put our conceptual machines to use in defining arithmetical operations on counting numbers.

13.1 Hyperoperations

13.1.1 – By convention, successive arithmetic operations are defined as *hyperoperations*, beginning with the successor function, H_0, defined previously in §11.2.5 as:

$$H_0(n) \equiv C(\{\text{«num»}, n\})$$

13.1.2 – In this view of mathematical hyperoperations, each successive hyperoperation is denoted by incrementing the subscript, with the semantic interpretion of each as a repetition of the previous hyperoperation.

13.1.3 – For example, addition, $H_1(a, b)$, can be seen as repeated application of the successor function. Multiplication, $H_2(a, b)$, can be seen as repeated application of the addition function. Exponentiation, $H_3(a, b)$, can be seen as repeated application of the multiplication function. Beyond exponentiation, the pattern holds with a fourth operation known as *tetration*, a fifth called *pentation*, and so forth.

13.1.4 – There are a few caveats here. 0 is used as the identity before any successive operations are applied under H_1, while 1 is used as the identity for all subsequent operations.

13.1.5 – For example:

$$H_1(x, 0) = x + 0 = x$$
$$H_2(x, 1) = x \times 1 = x$$
$$H_3(x, 1) = x^1 = x$$
$$H_4(x, 1) = x$$
$$H_5(x, 1) = x$$

13.1.6 – Whereas:

$$H_1(x, 1) = x + 1 = H_0(x)$$
$$H_2(x, 0) = x \times 0 = 0$$
$$H_3(x, 0) = x^0 = 1$$
$$H_4(x, 0) = 1$$
$$H_5(x, 0) = 1$$

13.1.7 – In this chapter we will implement machines to represent these hyperoperations (and their inverses) on counting numbers.

13.2 Addition

13.2.1 – As noted, addition can be thought of as the repeated application of the successor function, with zero as the identity. Let's implement this operation as a new machine, $\mathcal{M}_{1_c}$.

13.2.2 – Our machine specifier σ_{0_c} will hold three parameters: «op1», «op2», and «sum».

$$\sigma_{1_c}(o_1, o_2, r) = \Big\langle \langle \text{«op1»}, o_1 \rangle, \ \langle \text{«op2»}, o_2 \rangle, \ \langle \text{«sum»}, r \rangle \Big\rangle$$

13.2.3 – Our first state copies «op1» to «sum» and replaces it with [ ] when «sum» is the proxy:

$$s_{0_{c1}} = \sigma_{1_c}\Big([\,], \ [\,], \ [\cdot]\Big)$$

$$R(s_{0_{c1}}) \to \sigma_{1_c}\Big([\,], \ s_{0_{c1}}[\text{op2}], \ s_{0_{c1}}[\text{op1}]\Big)$$

13.2.4 – Our second state matches the machine when «op2» is greater than «0»:

$$s_{1_{c1}} = \sigma_{1_c}\Big([\cdot], \ \text{«not-0»}, \ [\,]\Big)$$

$$R(s_{1_{c1}}) \to \sigma_{1_c}\Big([\,], \ H_0^{-1}(s_{1_{c1}}[\text{op2}]), \ H_0(s_{1_{c1}}[\text{sum}])\Big)$$

13.2.5 – We can see that this relation simply subtracts one from «op2» and adds it to «sum».

13.2.6 – Our final state cleans up, leaving only the result in «sum»:

$$s_{2_{c1}} = \sigma_{1_c}\Big([\cdot], \ \text{«}\dot{0}\text{»}, \ [\,]\Big)$$

$$R(s_{2_{c1}}) \to \sigma_{1_c}\Big([\,], \ [\,], \ s_{2_{c1}}[\text{sum}]\Big)$$

13.2.7 – Now our machine specifier:

$$\mathcal{M}_{1_c}(o_1, o_2) \equiv \sigma_{1_c}\Big(o_1, o_2, [\,]\Big)$$

13.2.8 – And our operation:

$$H_{1_c}(o_1, o_2) \equiv X\Big(R(\mathcal{M}_{1_c}(o_1, o_2)), \text{«sum»}\Big)$$

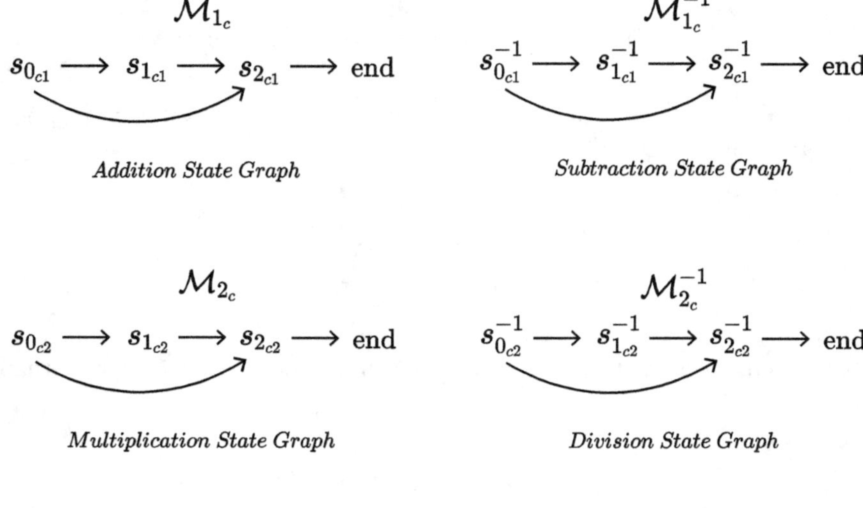

Figure 28: *Arithmetical Machine State Graphs:* Notice the similarities between the states of the hyperoperations above. In later chapters, we will explore how we can generalize these similarities.

13.2.9 – Note the general structure of the instructions below. There will be general patterns that occur in following hyperoperations.

13.2.10 – This will become of significant importance later in the book, when we create machines that generalize other machines, and in fact build a machine that generalizes hyperoperations.

13.2.11 – Here's our addition instruction table:

	s	$R(s)$
$s_{0_{c1}}$		
«op1»	[ ]	[ ]
«op2»	[ ]	$s_{0_{c1}}[\text{op2}]$
«sum»	[·]	$s_{0_{c1}}[\text{op1}]$
$s_{1_{c1}}$		
«op1»	[·]	[ ]
«op2»	«not-0»	$H_0^{-1}(s_{1_{c1}}[\text{op2}])$
«sum»	[ ]	$H_0(s_{1_{c1}}[\text{sum}])$
$s_{2_{c1}}$		
«op1»	[·]	[ ]
«op2»	«$\dot{0}$»	[ ]
«sum»	[ ]	$s_{2_{c1}}[\text{sum}]$

13.2.12 – Illustrated with $\mathcal{M}_{1_c}(\text{«4»}, \text{«3»})$, we expect a «sum» of «7»:

	«op1»	«op2»	«sum»
$\mathcal{M}_{1_c}(\text{«4»}, \text{«3»})$	«4»	«3»	[ ]
$R(s_{0_{c1}}) \rightarrow s_{1_{c1}}$	[ ]	«3»	«4»
$R(s_{1_{c1}}) \rightarrow s_{1_{c1}}$	[ ]	«2»	«5»
$R(s_{1_{c1}}) \rightarrow s_{1_{c1}}$	[ ]	«1»	«6»
$R(s_{1_{c1}}) \rightarrow s_{2_{c1}}$	[ ]	«0»	«7»
$R(s_{2_{c1}})$	[ ]	[ ]	«7»

13.3 Multiplication

13.3.1 – Now we can use our new addition operation, $H_{1_c}(o_1, o_2)$, to define a multiplication machine through relational composition.

13.3.2 – Our specifier σ_{2_c} takes 3 arguments, «op1», «op2», and «product».

$$\sigma_{2_c}(o_1, o_2, r) = \Big\langle \langle \text{«op1»}, o_1 \rangle,\ \langle \text{«op2»}, o_2 \rangle,\ \langle \text{«product»}, r \rangle \Big\rangle$$

13.3.3 – Our first state $s_{0_{c2}}$ sets «product» to «0»:

$$s_{0_{c2}} = \sigma_{2_c}\Big([\,], [\,], [\cdot]\Big)$$

$$R(s_{0_{c2}}) \to \sigma_{2_c}\Big(s_{0_{c2}}[\text{op1}],\ s_{0_{c2}}[\text{op2}],\ \text{«0»}\Big)$$

13.3.4 – Our second state adds «op1» to «sum» and decrements «op2», so long as «op2» is greater than «0»:

$$s_{1_{c2}} = \sigma_{2_c}\Big([\,], \text{«not-0»}, [\,]\Big)$$

$$R(s_{1_{c2}}) \to \sigma_{2_c}\Big(s_{1_{c2}}[\text{op1}],\ H_0^{-1}(s_{1_{c2}}[\text{op2}]),\ H_{1_c}(s_{1_{c2}}[\text{product}], s_{1_{c2}}[\text{op1}])\Big)$$

13.3.5 – Notice the reference here back to our addition operation H_{1_c}.

13.3.6 – Our final state resets «op1» and «op2» to $[\,]$, leaving only «product», when «op2» is equal to «0».

$$s_{2_{c2}} = \sigma_{2_c}\Big([\,], \text{«}\dot{0}\text{»}, [\,]\Big)$$

$$R(s_{2_{c2}}) \to \sigma_{2_c}\Big([\,],\ [\,],\ s_{2_{c2}}[\text{product}]\Big)$$

13.3.7 – Below we define our machine specifier $\mathcal{M}_{2_c}$:

$$\mathcal{M}_{2_c}(o_1, o_2) \equiv \sigma_{2_c}\Big(o_1, o_2, [\,]\Big)$$

13.3.8 – And our operation H_{2_c}:

$$H_{2_c}(o_1, o_2) \equiv X\Big(R(\mathcal{M}_{2_c}(o_1, o_2)), \text{«product»}\Big)$$

13.3.9 – Let's illustrate $2 \times 3 = 6$ with $\mathcal{M}_{2_c}(\text{«2»}, \text{«3»})$:

	«op1»	«op2»	«product»
$\mathcal{M}_{2_c}(\text{«2», «3»})$	«2»	«3»	[ ]
$R(s_{0_{c2}}) \to s_{2_{c1}}$	«2»	«3»	«0»
$R(s_{2_{c1}}) \to s_{2_{c1}}$	«2»	«2»	«2»
$R(s_{2_{c1}}) \to s_{2_{c1}}$	«2»	«1»	«4»
$R(s_{2_{c1}}) \to s_{2_{c2}}$	«2»	«0»	«6»
$R(s_{2_{c2}})$	[ ]	[ ]	«6»

13.4 Exponentiation

13.4.1 – Similarly, we can utilize our multiplication operation, $H_{2_c}(o_1, o_2)$, to define an exponentiation machine.

13.4.2 – Our specifier σ_{3_c} takes 3 arguments, «op1», «op2», and «power».

$$\sigma_{3_c}(o_1, o_2, r) = \Big\langle \langle \text{«op1»}, o_1 \rangle,\ \langle \text{«op2»}, o_2 \rangle,\ \langle \text{«power»}, r \rangle \Big\rangle$$

13.4.3 – Our first state, sets «power» to «1»:

$$s_{0_{c3}} = \sigma_{3_c}\Big([\,], [\,], [\cdot] \Big)$$

$$R(s_{0_{c3}}) \to \sigma_{3_c}\Big(s_{0_{c3}}[\text{op1}],\ s_{0_{c3}}[\text{op2}],\ \text{«1»} \Big)$$

13.4.4 – Our second state multiplies «power» by «op1» and decrements «op2», so long as «op2» is greater than «0»:

$$s_{1_{c3}} = \sigma_{3_c}\Big([\,], \text{«not-0»}, [\,] \Big)$$

$$R(s_{1_{c3}}) \to \sigma_{3_c}\Big(s_{1_{c3}}[\text{op1}],\ H_0^{-1}(s_{1_{c3}}[\text{op2}]),\ H_{2_c}(s_{1_{c3}}[\text{power}], s_{1_{c3}}[\text{op1}]) \Big)$$

13.4.5 – Notice the usage here of our multiplication operation, H_{2_c}.

13.4.6 – And finally we reset «op1» and «op2» to [ ], leaving only «power», when «op2» is equal to «0».

$$s_{2_{c3}} = \sigma_{3_c}\Big([\,], \text{«}\dot{0}\text{»}, [\,] \Big)$$

$$R(s_{2_{c3}}) \to \sigma_{3_c}([\,],\ [\,],\ s_{2_{c3}}[\text{power}])$$

13.4.7 – Below we have our machine specifier and operation:

$$\mathcal{M}_{3_c}(o_1, o_2) \equiv \sigma_{3_c}\Big(o_1, o_2, [\,]\Big)$$

$$H_{3_c}(o_1, o_2) \equiv X\Big(R(\mathcal{M}_{3_c}(o_1, o_2)), \text{«power»}\Big)$$

13.4.8 – Let's demonstrate 3^4 with $\mathcal{M}_{3_c}(\text{«3»}, \text{«4»})$:

	«op1»	«op2»	«power»
$\mathcal{M}_{3_c}(\text{«3»}, \text{«4»})$	«3»	«4»	[ ]
$R(s_{0_{c3}}) \rightarrow s_{1_{c3}}$	«3»	«4»	«1»
$R(s_{1_{c3}}) \rightarrow s_{1_{c3}}$	«3»	«3»	«3»
$R(s_{1_{c3}}) \rightarrow s_{1_{c3}}$	«3»	«2»	«9»
$R(s_{1_{c3}}) \rightarrow s_{1_{c3}}$	«3»	«1»	«27»
$R(s_{1_{c3}}) \rightarrow s_{2_{c3}}$	«3»	«0»	«81»
$R(s_{2_{c3}})$	[ ]	[ ]	«81»

13.5 Subtraction

13.5.1 – Now that we've built up the first few hyperoperations, it would also be useful to demonstrate how to construct their inverses. Let's specify our first inverse, H_1^{-1}, subtraction.

13.5.2 – Similar to addition, subtraction can be seen in terms of repeated applications of H_0^{-1}.

13.5.3 – Our machine specifier $\sigma_{1_c}^{-1}$ will hold «op1», «op2», and «diff».

$$\sigma_{1_c}^{-1}(o_1, o_2, r, q) = \Big\langle \langle \text{«op1»}, o_1 \rangle, \ \langle \text{«op2»}, o_2 \rangle, \ \langle \text{«diff»}, r \rangle \Big\rangle$$

13.5.4 – Our first state copies «op1» to «diff» and replaces it with [ ] when «sum» is the proxy and the operands are any two valid numbers. We will introduce the new notation «any-num», which is equivalent to «0» (the concept that matches any counting number):

$$s_{0_{c1}}^{-1} = \sigma_{1_c}^{-1}\Big(\text{«any-num»}, \text{«any-num»}, [\cdot]\Big)$$

$$R(s_{0_{c1}}^{-1}) \rightarrow \sigma_{1_c}^{-1}\Big([\,], \ s_{0_{c1}}^{-1}[\text{op2}], \ s_{0_{c1}}^{-1}[\text{op1}]\Big)$$

13.5.5 – Our second state decrements «op2» and «diff», so long as «op2» and «diff» are greater than «0»:

$$s_{1_{c1}}^{-1} = \sigma_{1_c}^{-1}\Big([\cdot], \text{«not-0»}, \text{«not-0»}\Big)$$

$$R(s_{1_{c1}}^{-1}) \rightarrow \sigma_{1_c}^{-1}\Big([\,], \; H_0^{-1}(s_{1_{c1}}^{-1}[\text{op2}]), \; H_0^{-1}(s_{1_{c1}}^{-1}[\text{diff}])\Big)$$

13.5.6 – Our third state cleans up the state, leaving only the result in «diff»:

$$s_{2_{c1}}^{-1} = \sigma_{1_c}^{-1}\Big([\cdot], \text{«}\dot{0}\text{»}, [\,]\Big)$$

$$R(s_{2_{c1}}^{-1}) \rightarrow \sigma_{1_c}^{-1}\Big([\,], \; [\,], \; s_{2_{c1}}^{-1}[\text{diff}]\Big)$$

13.5.7 – Our fourth state cleans up the state in the case of a negative number, leaving only the difference in «op2»:

$$s_{3_{c1}}^{-1} = \sigma_{1_c}^{-1}\Big([\cdot], [\,], \text{«}\dot{0}\text{»}\Big)$$

$$R(s_{3_{c1}}^{-1}) \rightarrow \sigma_{1_c}^{-1}\Big([\,], \; s_{3_{c1}}^{-1}[\text{op2}], \; [\,]\Big)$$

13.5.8 – Let's illustrate with $\mathcal{M}_{1_c}^{-1}(\text{«4»}, \text{«3»})$. We would expect «diff» = «1»:

	«op1»	«op2»	«diff»
$\mathcal{M}_{1_c}^{-1}(\text{«4»}, \text{«3»})$	«4»	«3»	[ ]
$R(s_{0_{c1}}^{-1}) \rightarrow s_{1_{c1}}^{-1}$	[ ]	«3»	«4»
$R(s_{1_{c1}}^{-1}) \rightarrow s_{1_{c1}}^{-1}$	[ ]	«2»	«3»
$R(s_{1_{c1}}^{-1}) \rightarrow s_{1_{c1}}^{-1}$	[ ]	«1»	«2»
$R(s_{1_{c1}}^{-1}) \rightarrow s_{2_{c1}}^{-1}$	[ ]	«0»	«1»
$R(s_{2_{c1}}^{-1})$	[ ]	[ ]	«1»

13.5.9 – Note that if at any point «op2» > «0» and «diff» = «0», the machine would fall into an invalid state when H_0^{-1} is applied to «diff»'s «0». A proxy would be left in «diff», with a value one fewer than the remaining number in «op2».

13.5.10 – This feature of a proxy resulting as the operation's «diff» has important uses in the division machine.

13.5.11 – First, recall the definition of zero from §11.2.2:

$$\text{«}0_c\text{»} \equiv \langle\text{«num»},[\,]\rangle$$

13.5.12 – Along with the definition of H_0^{-1} from §11.3:

$$H_0^{-1}(n) \equiv X(\langle n\rangle, \text{«num»})$$

13.5.13 – In order to avoid this outcome, we only decrement so long as «diff» > «0». When «0» remains in «diff» with a numeric value in «op2», the value in «op2» represents the remainder, *a negative number.*

13.5.14 – Let's try again with $\mathcal{M}_{1_c}^{-1}(\text{«}3\text{»}, \text{«}5\text{»})$, with an expected "remainder" of «2» (representing -2) in «op2»:

	«op1»	«op2»	«diff»
$\mathcal{M}_{1_c}^{-1}(\text{«}3\text{»}, \text{«}5\text{»})$	«3»	«5»	[ ]
$R(s_{0_{c1}}^{-1}) \to s_{1_{c1}}^{-1}$	[ ]	«5»	«3»
$R(s_{1_{c1}}^{-1}) \to s_{1_{c1}}^{-1}$	[ ]	«4»	«2»
$R(s_{1_{c1}}^{-1}) \to s_{1_{c1}}^{-1}$	[ ]	«3»	«1»
$R(s_{1_{c1}}^{-1}) \to s_{3_{c1}}^{-1}$	[ ]	«2»	«0»
$R(s_{3_{c1}}^{-1})$	[ ]	«2»	[ ]

13.5.15 – We will put to use an operation for subtraction:

$$H_1^{-1}(o_1, o_2) \equiv X\big(R(\mathcal{M}_{1_c}^{-1}(o_1, o_2)), \text{«diff»}\big)$$

13.6 Division

13.6.1 – If you look back through the subtraction machine outlined in §13.5 and the addition machine from §13.2, the only significant difference is that is in $R(s_{1_{c1}})$ and $R(s_{1_{c1}}^{-1})$, instead of H_0 being applied to the result in «sum», H_0^{-1} is applied to the result in «diff» instead.

13.6.2 – We can fashion other inverses of our hyperoperations in a similar manner. In division, we will repeatedly subtract from the given value.

13.6.3 – Let's start with our machine specifier, which has four components «op1», «op2», «next», and «quot»:

$$\sigma_{2_c}^{-1}(o_1, o_2, n, r) = \Big\langle \langle \text{«op1»}, o_1 \rangle, \ \langle \text{«op2»}, o_2 \rangle, \ \langle \text{«next»}, n \rangle, \ \langle \text{«quot»}, r \rangle \Big\rangle$$

13.6.4 – Our first state will simply convert the proxy in «quot» to «0» and will set «next» to «op1» minus «op2». This term will keep track of the number of times we have subtracted the divisor from the dividend:

$$s_{0_{c2}}^{-1} = \sigma_{2_c}^{-1}\Big([\,], [\,], [\,], [\cdot]\Big)$$

$$R(s_{0_{c2}}^{-1}) \to \sigma_{2_c}^{-1}\Big(s_{0_{c2}}^{-1}[\text{op1}], \ s_{0_{c2}}^{-1}[\text{op2}],$$
$$H_1^{-1}(s_{0_{c2}}^{-1}[\text{op1}], s_{0_{c2}}^{-1}[\text{op2}]), \ \text{«0»}\Big)$$

13.6.5 – Next we increment «quot» so long as «next» is a valid number:

$$s_{2_{c1}}^{-1} = \sigma_{2_c}^{-1}\Big([\,], [\,], \text{«any-num»}, [\,]\Big)$$

$$R(s_{2_{c1}}^{-1}) \to \sigma_{2_c}^{-1}\Big(H_1^{-1}(s_{2_{c1}}^{-1}[\text{op1}], s_{2_{c1}}^{-1}[\text{op2}]), \ s_{2_{c1}}^{-1}[\text{op2}],$$
$$H_1^{-1}(s_{2_{c1}}^{-1}[\text{next}], s_{2_{c1}}^{-1}[\text{op2}]), \ H_0(s_{2_{c1}}^{-1}[\text{quot}])\Big)$$

13.6.6 – Finally, when our «next» value becomes invalid (i.e. turns to proxy), we clean up the operation. Any remaining value in «op1» is the remainder, while «quot» is the quotient:

$$s_{2_{c2}}^{-1} = \sigma_{2_c}^{-1}\Big([\,], [\,], [\cdot], \text{«any-num»}\Big)$$

$$R(s_{2_{c2}}^{-1}) \to \sigma_{2_c}^{-1}\Big(s_{2_{c2}}^{-1}[\text{op1}], \ [\,], \ [\,], \ s_{2_{c2}}^{-1}[\text{quot}]\Big)$$

13.6.7 – First, let's look at numbers that divide evenly, say 6/2:

	«op1»	«op2»	«next»	«quot»
$\mathcal{M}_{2_c}^{-1}(\text{«6»}, \text{«2»})$	«6»	«2»	[ ]	[ ]
$R(s_{2_{c1}}^{-1}) \to s_{2_{c1}}^{-1}$	«6»	«2»	«4»	«0»
$R(s_{2_{c1}}^{-1}) \to s_{2_{c1}}^{-1}$	«4»	«2»	«2»	«1»
$R(s_{2_{c1}}^{-1}) \to s_{2_{c1}}^{-1}$	«2»	«2»	«0»	«2»
$R(s_{2_{c1}}^{-1}) \to s_{2_{c2}}^{-1}$	«0»	«2»	[ ]	«3»
$R(s_{2_{c2}}^{-1})$	«0»	[ ]	[ ]	«3»

13.6.8 – And now we can look at an example with a non-zero remainder, 10/3:

	«op1»	«op2»	«next»	«quot»
$\mathcal{M}_{2_c}^{-1}(\text{«10»}, \text{«3»})$	«10»	«3»	[ ]	[ ]
$R(s_{0_{c2}}^{-1}) \to s_{2_{c1}}^{-1}$	«10»	«3»	«7»	«0»
$R(s_{2_{c1}}^{-1}) \to s_{2_{c1}}^{-1}$	«7»	«3»	«4»	«1»
$R(s_{2_{c1}}^{-1}) \to s_{2_{c1}}^{-1}$	«4»	«3»	«1»	«2»
$R(s_{2_{c1}}^{-1}) \to s_{2_{c2}}^{-1}$	«1»	«3»	[ ]	«3»
$R(s_{2_{c2}}^{-1})$	«1»	[ ]	[ ]	«3»

13.7 Further Operations

13.7.1 – Machines to implement further hyperoperations, including tetration and beyond, are easily imaginable and implementable following the same patterns we've demonstrated in this chapter. We will revisit a generalization of them in §22 by constructing a machine that builds other machines.

13.7.2 – The same applies to further inverse operations, but we do not treat them further in this book.

13.7.3 – One thing to note about inverse operations is that after division, there are *two* inverse operations for each hyperoperation.

13.7.4 – This is because operations past multiplication, H_2, are no longer commutative; the inverse to be applied depends on the operand of the original operation you'd like to retrieve.

13.7.5 – For example, exponentiation has two inverses: logarithms to retrieve the power given its base, and roots to retrieve the base given its power.

14 Binary Machines

"I see no limit to the capabilities of machines."

— Claude Shannon

In this chapter, we construct a machine to produce our first digital numeric representations: binary numbers.

14.1 Binary Numbers

14.1.1 – We can now describe our first complex conceptual system: the construction of a binary number from a counting number.

14.1.2 – We begin by defining our *machine*, $\mathcal{M}_b$, in terms of our state specifier σ_b:

$$\sigma_b(s, v, c, i, d) \equiv$$

$$\Big\langle \langle\text{«state»}, s\rangle, \langle\text{«value»}, v\rangle, \langle\text{«current»}, c\rangle, \langle\text{«index»}, i\rangle, \langle\text{«digits»}, d\rangle \Big\rangle$$

$$\Upsilon(\{\text{«begin»}, \text{«iter»}, \text{«carry»}, \text{«end»}\}, \quad \text{«state»})$$

$$\Upsilon(\text{«digits»}, \text{«sequence»})$$

$$\Upsilon(\{\text{«index»}, \text{«current»}, \text{«value»}\}, \text{«num»})$$

14.1.3 – Let's define our initial state. It is labeled as «begin» and uses [ ] in «value» as a placeholder for the input counting number we want to convert to binary.

$$s_{0_b} = \sigma_b\Big(\text{«begin»},\ [\,],\ [\,],\ [\,],\ [\,]\Big)$$

$$R(s_{0_b}) \to \sigma_b\Big(\text{«iter»},\ s_{0_b}[\text{value}],\ \text{«0»},\ \text{«0»},\ \langle\,\rangle\Big)$$

14.1.4 – Now we define our iterative states. s_{1_b} will represent the «iter» state in which the «current» digit is «0». In this circumstance, we only increment the «current» value, referenced by «index» in «digits».

$$s_{1_b} = \sigma_b\Big(\text{«iter»},\ \text{«not-0»},\ \text{«}\dot{0}\text{»},\ [\,],\ [\,]\Big)$$

14.1.5 – Note that a dot over a digit, such as «$\dot{0}$» in s_{1_b}, is used to force the concepts to match the value specified exactly, as opposed to that value and any larger values. This is described in §8.4.7.

$$R(s_{1_b}) \to \sigma_b\Big(\text{«iter»},\ H_0^{-1}(s_{1_b}[\text{value}]),\ \text{«1»},$$

$$s_{1_b}[\text{index}],\ T(s_{1_b}[\text{digits}],\ s_{1_b}[\text{index}],\ \text{«1»})\Big)$$

14.1.6 – s_{2_b} will represent the «iter» state in which the «current» digit is «1». In this circumstance, we set «state» to «carry» and increment «index».

$$s_{2_b} = \sigma_b\Big(\text{«iter»},\ \text{«not-0»},\ \text{«}\dot{1}\text{»},\ [\,],\ [\,] \Big)$$

$$R(s_{2_b}) \rightarrow \sigma_b\Big(\text{«carry»},\ \ s_{2_b}[\text{value}],\ \ s_{2_b}[\text{digits}][H_0(s_{2_b}[\text{index}])],$$
$$H_0(s_{2_b}[\text{index}]),\ \ T(s_{2_b}[\text{digits}],\ s_{2_b}[\text{index}],\ \text{«0»}) \Big)$$

14.1.7 – Keep in mind that all extractions performed on «sequence»'s— «digits» in this case as $s_{2_b}[\text{digits}][H_0(s_{2_b}[\text{index}])]$—should be interpreted as X', returning «0» when no match is found.

14.1.8 – s_{3_b} will represent the «carry» state in which the «current» digit is «1». In this circumstance, we set the «current» value to «0», referenced by «index» in «digits», and increment «index» (and repeat until «current» becomes «0»).

$$s_{3_b} = \sigma_b\Big(\text{«carry»},\ \text{«not-0»},\ \text{«}\dot{1}\text{»},\ [\,],\ [\,] \Big)$$

$$R(s_{3_b}) \rightarrow \sigma_b\Big(\text{«carry»},\ \ s_{3_b}[\text{value}],\ \ s_{3_b}[\text{digits}][H_0(s_{3_b}[\text{index}])],$$
$$H_0(s_{3_b}[\text{index}]),\ \ T(s_{3_b}[\text{digits}],\ s_{3_b}[\text{index}],\ \text{«0»}), \Big)$$

14.1.9 – s_{4_b} will represent the «carry» state in which the «current» digit is «0». In this circumstance, we increment the «current» value to «1», and reset «state» to «iter» and «index» to «0».

$$s_{4_b} = \sigma_b\Big(\text{«carry»},\ \text{«not-0»},\ \text{«}\dot{0}\text{»},\ [\,],\ [\,] \Big)$$

$$R(s_{4_b}) \rightarrow \sigma_b\Big(\text{«iter»},\ \ H_0^{-1}(s_{2_b}[\text{value}]),\ \ s_{4_b}[\text{digits}][0],$$
$$\text{«0»},\ \ T(s_{4_b}[\text{digits}],\ s_{4_b}[\text{index}],\ \text{«1»}) \Big)$$

14.1.10 – This returns the machine to the state representation by s_{1_b} and continues adding each digit, one by one, until «value» is decreased to «0».

14.1.11 – When our «value» is finally decreased to «0», we move to the «end» state, with our final value in [digits].

$$s_{5_b} = \sigma_b\Big(\text{«iter»},\ \text{«}\dot{0}\text{»},\ [\,],\ [\,],\ [\,] \Big)$$

$$R(s_{5_b}) \rightarrow \sigma_b\Big(\text{«end»},\ [\,],\ [\,],\ [\,],\ s_{5_b}[\text{digits}] \Big)$$

14.1.12 – This machine is more complicated than those we've built up to this point.

14.1.13 – For legibility, let's take a look at the instruction table:

	s	$R(s)$
s_{0_b}		
«state»	«begin»	«iter»
«value»	[ ]	$s_{0_b}[\text{value}]$
«current»	[ ]	«0»
«index»	[ ]	«0»
«digits»	[ ]	$\langle\,\rangle$
s_{1_b}		
«state»	«iter»	«iter»
«value»	«not-0»	$H_0^{-1}(s_{1_b}[\text{value}])$
«current»	«$\dot{0}$»	«1»
«index»	[ ]	$s_{1_b}[\text{index}]$
«digits»	[ ]	$T(s_{1_b}[\text{digits}],\ s_{1_b}[\text{index}],\ «1»)$
s_{2_b}		
«state»	«iter»	«carry»
«value»	«not-0»	$s_{2_b}[\text{value}]$
«current»	«$\dot{1}$»	$s_{2_b}[\text{digits}][H_0(s_{2_b}[\text{index}])]$
«index»	[ ]	$H_0(s_{2_b}[\text{index}])$
«digits»	[ ]	$T(s_{2_b}[\text{digits}],\ s_{2_b}[\text{index}],\ «0»)$
s_{3_b}		
«state»	«carry»	«carry»
«value»	«not-0»	$s_{3_b}[\text{value}]$
«current»	«$\dot{1}$»	$s_{3_b}[\text{digits}][H_0(s_{3_b}[\text{index}])]$
«index»	[ ]	$H_0(s_{3_b}[\text{index}])$
«digits»	[ ]	$T(s_{3_b}[\text{digits}],\ s_{3_b}[\text{index}],\ «0»)$
s_{4_b}		
«state»	«carry»	«iter»

	s	$R(s)$
«value»	«not-0»	$H_0^{-1}(s_{4_b}[\text{value}])$
«current»	«0̇»	$s_{4_b}[\text{digits}][0]$
«index»	[ ]	«0»
«digits»	[ ]	$T(s_{4_b}[\text{digits}],\ s_{4_b}[\text{index}],\ «1»)$
s_{5_b}		
«state»	«iter»	«end»
«value»	«0»	[ ]
«current»	[ ]	[ ]
«index»	[ ]	[ ]
«digits»	[ ]	$s_{5_b}[\text{digits}]$

14.1.14 – Below is an evaluation table of our machine calculating the binary representation of «4».

14.1.15 – Note that we have shortened our representation of «digits» to omit the index, and to show the value with the largest «index» first, in order to make it read like the standard representation of a binary number.

	«state»	«value»	«current»	«index»	«digits»
	«begin»	«4»	[ ]	[ ]	[ ]
$R(s_{0_b}) \to s_{1_b}$	«iter»	«4»	«0»	«0»	$\langle\,\rangle$
$R(s_{1_b}) \to s_{2_b}$	«iter»	«3»	«1»	«0»	$\langle«1»\rangle$
$R(s_{2_b}) \to s_{4_b}$	«carry»	«3»	«0»	«1»	$\langle«0»\rangle$
$R(s_{4_b}) \to s_{1_b}$	«iter»	«2»	«0»	«0»	$\langle«1», «0»\rangle$
$R(s_{1_b}) \to s_{2_b}$	«iter»	«1»	«1»	«0»	$\langle«1», «1»\rangle$
$R(s_{2_b}) \to s_{3_b}$	«carry»	«1»	«0»	«1»	$\langle«1», «0»\rangle$
$R(s_{3_b}) \to s_{4_b}$	«carry»	«1»	«0»	«2»	$\langle«0», «0»\rangle$
$R(s_{4_b}) \to s_{5_b}$	«iter»	«0»	«0»	«0»	$\langle«1», «0», «0»\rangle$
	«end»	[ ]	[ ]	[ ]	$\langle«1», «0», «0»\rangle$

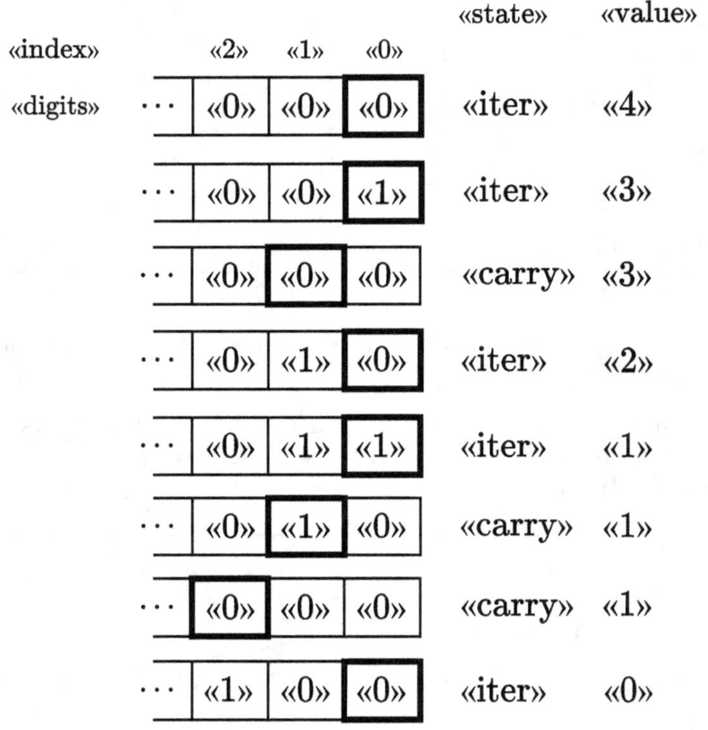

Figure 29: *Binary Machine Illustrated*: This graphic illustrates the significant states of the machine $\mathcal{M}_b(«4»)$. The bolded square indicates the «current» value and «index». Notice the «carry» pattern that overwrites «1»'s with «0»'s until the first «0» is found.

14.1.16 – This examples shows, step by step, each transformation in the machine's state from s_{0_b} through the final result, with «digits» as $\langle$«1», «0», «0»$\rangle$, the binary representation of «4».

14.1.17 – As a shorthand, we can represent binary numbers with a subscript b, e.g. «4_b».

14.2 Binary Successor Machine

14.2.1 – Now we can define a simple machine that gives the successor of a binary number:

$$\mathcal{M}_{0_b}(d) \equiv \mathcal{M}_b(\text{«1»}, d)$$

14.2.2 – The above machine sets the initial state of the machine to the digits represented by d, and adds «1» to the resulting value.

14.2.3 – For convenience, we'll define an operation to make utilization of the previous machine easier:

$$H_{0_b}(d) \equiv R(\mathcal{M}_{0_b}(d))[\text{digits}]$$

14.2.4 – Notice we use operation R to produce the resultant state and [digits] to extract the digits from the resulting object.

14.2.5 – In action:

$$H_{0_b}(\langle\text{«0»}\rangle) \to \langle\text{«1»}\rangle$$

$$H_{0_b}(\langle\text{«1»}\rangle) \to \langle\text{«1»}, \text{«0»}\rangle$$

$$H_{0_b}(\langle\text{«1»}, \text{«0»}, \text{«1»}\rangle) \to \langle\text{«1»}, \text{«1»}, \text{«0»}\rangle$$

14.3 Binary Anti-Successor Machine

14.3.1 – The antisuccessor operation H_0^{-1}, defined in §11.3, makes prominent appearances in many cognitive machines, including the arithmetical machines we defined in §13.2, §13.3, and §13.4.

14.3.2 – We will need a similar operation in order to create analogous arithmetical machines in binary.

14.3.3 – Note that the following machine is designed to make the process most clear, and can be optimized fairly trivially.

14.3.4 – First, we define the state specifier for our binary anti-successor machine, $\sigma_{0_b}^{-1}$:

$$\sigma_{0_b}^{-1}(s, c, i, d) \equiv \Big\langle \langle\text{«state»}, s\rangle, \langle\text{«current»}, c\rangle, \langle\text{«index»}, i\rangle, \langle\text{«digits»}, d\rangle \Big\rangle$$

$$\Upsilon(\{\text{«begin»}, \text{«iter»}, \text{«carry»}, \text{«end»}\}, \quad \text{«state»})$$

$$\Upsilon(\text{«digits»}, \text{«sequence»})$$

$$\Upsilon(\{\text{«index»}, \text{«current»}\}, \text{«num»})$$

14.3.5 – Our first state initializes «current» to the least significant digit in «digits» and «index» to «0».

$$s_{0_{b0}}^{-1} = \sigma_{0_b}^{-1}\Big(\text{«begin»}, \; [\,], \; [\,], \; [\,]\Big)$$

$$R(s_{0_{b0}}^{-1}) \rightarrow \sigma_{0_b}^{-1}\Big(\text{«iter»}, \; s_{0_{b0}}^{-1}[\text{digits}][0], \; \text{«0»}, \; s_{0_{b0}}^{-1}[\text{digits}]\Big)$$

14.3.6 – If «current» at «index» «0» is equal to «1», change it to «0» and «end»:

$$s_{1_{b0}}^{-1} = \sigma_{0_b}^{-1}\Big(\text{«iter»}, \; \text{«1»}, \; \text{«0»}, \; [\,]\Big)$$

$$R(s_{1_{b0}}^{-1}) \rightarrow \sigma_{0_b}^{-1}\Big(\text{«end»}, \; [\,], \; [\,], \; T(s_{1_{b0}}^{-1}[\text{digits}], \text{«0»}, \text{«0»})\Big)$$

14.3.7 – Otherwise we «iter» up the tree so long as «current» is equal to «0»:

$$s_{2_{b0}}^{-1} = \sigma_{0_b}^{-1}\Big(\text{«iter»}, \; \text{«0»}, \; [\,], \; [\,]\Big)$$

$$R(s_{2_{b0}}^{-1}) \rightarrow \sigma_{0_b}^{-1}\Big(\text{«iter»}, \; s_{2_{b0}}^{-1}[\text{digits}][H_0(s_{2_{b0}}^{-1}[\text{index}])],$$
$$H_0(s_{2_{b0}}^{-1}[\text{index}]), \; s_{2_{b0}}^{-1}[\text{digits}]\Big)$$

14.3.8 – When a «1» is found we change it to «0» via operation T, then switch to «carry»:

$$s_{3_{b0}}^{-1} = \sigma_{0_b}^{-1}\Big(\text{«iter»}, \; \text{«1»}, \; [\,], \; [\,]\Big)$$

$$R(s_{3_{b0}}^{-1}) \rightarrow \sigma_{0_b}^{-1}\Big(\text{«carry»}, \; [\,], \; H_0^{-1}(s_{3_{b0}}^{-1}[\text{index}]),$$
$$T(s_{3_{b0}}^{-1}[\text{digits}], s_{3_{b0}}^{-1}[\text{index}], \text{«0»})\Big)$$

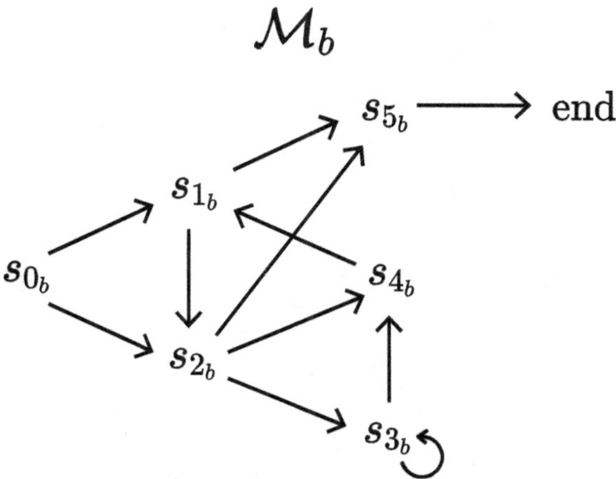

Figure 30: *Binary Machine State Graph:* Recall that s_{1_b} and s_{2_b} are our «iter» states, depending on whether the «current» digit is «0» or «1». s_{3_b} carries until a «0» is encountered, and s_{4_b} sets a carried «1» digit, and resets to s_{1_b}.

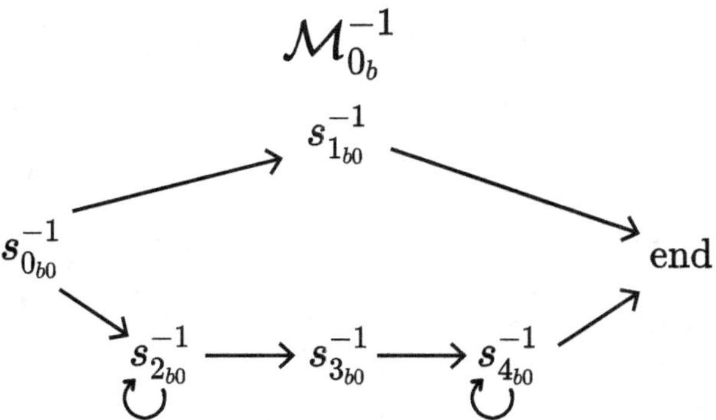

Figure 31: *Binary Anti-Successor Machine State Graph:* In this machine, $s_{1_{b0}}^{-1}$ shortcuts the mechanism if the first digit is «1». Otherwise, $s_{2_{b0}}^{-1}$ will keep incrementing which digit is «current» until it finds a «1». $s_{3_{b0}}^{-1}$ changes the «1» to «0», and $s_{4_{b0}}^{-1}$ traverses back down the digits, turning each «0» to «1» along the way.

14.3.9 – We then traverse «index» back down to «0», writing «1»'s along the way:

$$s_{4_{b0}}^{-1} = \sigma_{0_b}^{-1}\Big(\text{«carry»}, \; [\,], \; \text{«not-0»}, \; [\,]\Big)$$

$$R(s_{4_{b0}}^{-1}) \to \sigma_{0_b}^{-1}\Big(\text{«carry»}, \; [\,], \; H_0^{-1}(s_{4_{b0}}^{-1}[\text{index}]),$$
$$T(s_{4_{b0}}^{-1}[\text{digits}], s_{4_{b0}}^{-1}[\text{index}], \text{«1»})\Big)$$

14.3.10 – When reach «index» $=$ «0», we write a final «1» and switch to «end»:

$$s_{5_{b0}}^{-1} = \sigma_{0_b}^{-1}\Big(\text{«carry»}, \; [\,], \; \text{«}\dot{0}\text{»}, \; [\,]\Big)$$

$$R(s_{5_{b0}}^{-1}) \to \sigma_{0_b}^{-1}\Big(\text{«end»}, \; [\,], \; [\,], \; T(s_{5_{b0}}^{-1}[\text{digits}], \text{«0»}, \text{«1»})\Big)$$

14.3.11 – Let's demonstrate:

	«state»	«current»	«index»	«digits»
	«begin»	$[\,]$	$[\,]$	$\langle\text{«1»}, \text{«0»}, \text{«0»}\rangle$
$R(s_{0_{b0}}^{-1}) \to s_{2_{b0}}^{-1}$	«iter»	«0»	«0»	$\langle\text{«1»}, \text{«0»}, \text{«0»}\rangle$
$R(s_{2_{b0}}^{-1}) \to s_{3_{b0}}^{-1}$	«iter»	«0»	«1»	$\langle\text{«1»}, \text{«0»}, \text{«0»}\rangle$
$R(s_{3_{b0}}^{-1}) \to s_{4_{b0}}^{-1}$	«iter»	«1»	«2»	$\langle\text{«1»}, \text{«0»}, \text{«0»}\rangle$
$R(s_{4_{b0}}^{-1}) \to s_{4_{b0}}^{-1}$	«carry»	«0»	«1»	$\langle\text{«0»}, \text{«0»}, \text{«0»}\rangle$
$R(s_{4_{b0}}^{-1}) \to s_{5_{b0}}^{-1}$	«carry»	«0»	«0»	$\langle\text{«0»}, \text{«1»}, \text{«0»}\rangle$
$R(s_{5_{b0}}^{-1}) \to$	«end»	$[\,]$	$[\,]$	$\langle\text{«0»}, \text{«1»}, \text{«1»}\rangle$

14.3.12 – And we can verify that the given $100_2 = 4$ is one greater than the resulting $011_2 = 3$.

14.3.13 – Now let's define our machine specifier:

$$\mathcal{M}_{0_b}^{-1}(n) \equiv \sigma_{0_b}^{-1}(\text{«begin»}, [\,], [\,], n)$$

14.3.14 – And our operation, $H_{0_b}^{-1}(n)$:

$$H_{0_b}^{-1}(n) \equiv X\Big(R(\mathcal{M}_{0_b}^{-1}(n)), \text{«digits»}\Big)$$

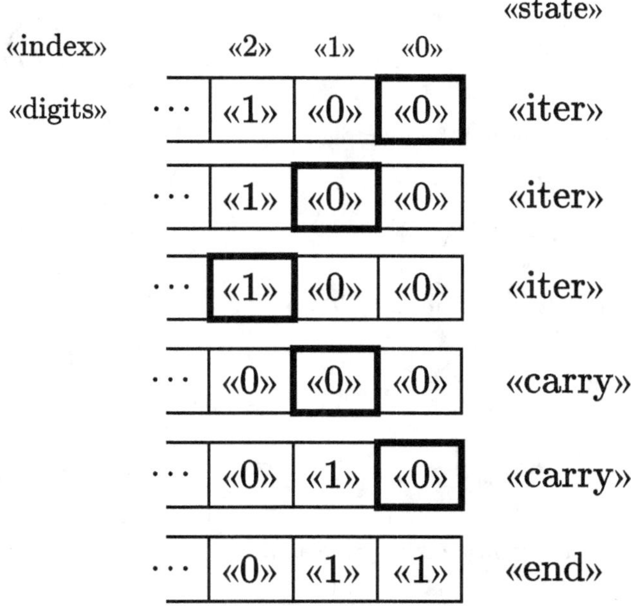

Figure 32: *Binary Anti-Successor Machine Illustrated*: This graphic illustrated the significant states of the machine $\mathcal{M}_{0b}^{-1}(\text{«4»})$. Notice that we increment «index» until we find the first «1». We change that digit to «0» and write «1»'s back down the sequence.

14.4 Binary Addition

14.4.1 – Similarly to §13, we can also define arithmetical operations on binary numbers. We do this by using essentially the same structure, but with our binary successor and anti-successor operations, H_{0_b} and $H_{0_b}^{-1}$, instead of H_0 and H_0^{-1}.

14.4.2 – Here we will demonstrate in terms of addition, but the same principles apply to any other arithmetical operation.

14.4.3 – Let's recall our counting addition state specifier from §13.2.2:

$$\sigma_{1_c}(o_1, o_2, r) = \Big\langle \langle \text{«op1»}, o_1 \rangle,\ \langle \text{«op2»}, o_2 \rangle,\ \langle \text{«sum»}, r \rangle \Big\rangle$$

14.4.4 – Our specifier will be identical:

$$\sigma_{1_b}(o_1, o_2, r) = \Big\langle \langle \text{«op1»}, o_1 \rangle,\ \langle \text{«op2»}, o_2 \rangle,\ \langle \text{«sum»}, r \rangle \Big\rangle$$

14.4.5 – Recall the first counting addition machine state from §13.2.3:

$$s_{0_{c1}} = \sigma_{1_c}\Big([\,], [\,], [\cdot]\Big)$$

$$R(s_{0_{c1}}) \to \sigma_{1_c}\Big([\,],\ s_{0_{c1}}[\text{op2}],\ s_{0_{c1}}[\text{op1}]\Big)$$

14.4.6 – Ours will again be nearly identical:

$$s_{1_{b0}} = \sigma_{1_b}\Big([\,], [\,], [\cdot]\Big)$$

$$R(s_{1_{b0}}) \to \sigma_{1_b}\Big([\,],\ s_{1_{b0}}[\text{op2}],\ s_{1_{b0}}[\text{op1}]\Big)$$

14.4.7 – Now let's look at the second state from the counting addition machine from §13.2.4:

$$s_{1_{c1}} = \sigma_{1_c}\Big([\cdot],\ \text{«not-0»},\ [\,]\Big)$$

$$R(s_{1_{c1}}) \to \sigma_{1_c}\Big([\,],\ H_0^{-1}(s_{1_{c1}}[\text{op2}]),\ H_0(s_{1_{c1}}[\text{sum}])\Big)$$

14.4.8 – There are a few terms in these formulae that need to be replaced so that they are amenable to use with binary numbers.

14.4.9 – To start, we need to replace «not-0» with $\langle\langle$«$\bar{0}$», «1»$\rangle\rangle$, the binary equivalent of «1».[14]

14.4.10 – We also need to replace all occurrences of H_0 and H_0^{-1} with H_{0_b} and $H_{0_b}^{-1}$, respectively.

14.4.11 – Applying those substitutions to the formula for the second state, we gather:

$$s_{1_{b1}} = \sigma_{1_b}\Big([\cdot],\ \langle\langle«\bar{0}», «1»\rangle\rangle,\ [\,]\Big)$$

$$R(s_{1_{b1}}) \to \sigma_{1_b}\Big([\,],\ H_{0_b}^{-1}(s_{1_{b1}}[\text{op2}]),\ H_{0_b}(s_{1_{b1}}[\text{sum}])\Big)$$

14.4.12 – For the third state from §13.2.6, we only need to substitute $\langle\langle$«$\bar{0}$», «$\dot{0}$»$\rangle\rangle$ for its counting equivalent «$\dot{0}$»:

$$s_{2_{b1}} = \sigma_{1_b}\Big([\cdot],\ \langle\langle«\bar{0}», «\dot{0}»\rangle\rangle,\ [\,]\Big)$$

$$R(s_{2_{b1}}) \to \sigma_{1_b}\Big([\,],\ [\,],\ s_{2_{b1}}[\text{sum}]\Big)$$

14.4.13 – Let's demonstrate with our example from §13.2.12, $4 + 3 = 7$:

	«op1»	«op2»	«sum»
	$\langle$«1», «0», «0»$\rangle$	$\langle$«0», «1», «1»$\rangle$	$[\,]$
$R(s_{1_{b0}}) \to s_{1_{b1}}$	$[\,]$	$\langle$«0», «1», «1»$\rangle$	$\langle$«1», «0», «0»$\rangle$
$R(s_{1_{b1}}) \to s_{1_{b1}}$	$[\,]$	$\langle$«0», «1», «0»$\rangle$	$\langle$«1», «0», «1»$\rangle$
$R(s_{1_{b1}}) \to s_{1_{b1}}$	$[\,]$	$\langle$«0», «0», «1»$\rangle$	$\langle$«1», «1», «0»$\rangle$
$R(s_{1_{b1}}) \to s_{2_{b1}}$	$[\,]$	$\langle$«0», «0», «0»$\rangle$	$\langle$«1», «1», «1»$\rangle$
$R(s_{2_{b1}})$	$[\,]$	$[\,]$	$\langle$«1», «1», «1»$\rangle$

14.4.14 – And, of course, $111_2 = 7$.

14.4.15 – We can easily imagine any other conversion of arithmetical hyperoperations from counting numbers to binary numbers following a similar procedure.

---

[14]From §12.5.8, «not-0» $\equiv$ «1».

14.5 Binary to Counting Number Conversion

14.5.1 – Using the mechanisms we've developed so far, we can also create a machine $\mathcal{M}_b^{-1}$, which takes a binary representation and converts it back to a counting number.

14.5.2 – First, our specifier:

$$\sigma_{bc}(d, l, i, v) \equiv \Big\langle \langle\text{«digits»}, d\rangle, \ \langle\text{«length»}, l\rangle, \ \langle\text{«index»}, i\rangle, \ \langle\text{«value»}, v\rangle \Big\rangle$$

14.5.3 – We need to include a «length», because a sequence does not contain information about the last place that a «1» value is held. There are probably better ways to represent this within the «digits» concept itself, but this structure will serve for our purposes.

14.5.4 – Our first state sets «index» to («length» -1)—because the «index» is zero-indexed—and sets our initial value to «0»:

$$s_{0_{bc}} = \sigma_{bc}([\,], [\,], [\,], [\cdot])$$

$$R(s_{0_{bc}}) \to \sigma_{bc}\Big(s_{0_{bc}}[\text{digits}], \ s_{0_{bc}}[\text{length}], \ H_0^{-1}(s_{0_{bc}}[\text{length}]), \ \text{«0»}\Big)$$

14.5.5 – Our second state takes the digit at «index» and multiplies it by $2^{\text{«index»}}$ to get the value of the position currently indicated by «index». It adds the result to «value», and decrements «index».

$$s_{1_{bc}} = \sigma_{bc}([\,], [\,], \text{«any-num»}, \text{«any-num»})$$

$$R(s_{1_{bc}}) \to \sigma_{bc}\Big(s_{1_{bc}}[\text{digits}], \ s_{1_{bc}}[\text{length}], \ H_0^{-1}(s_{1_{bc}}[\text{index}]),$$

$$H_{1_c}(s_{1_{bc}}[\text{value}], \ H_{2_c}(X(s_{1_{bc}}[\text{digits}], s_{1_{bc}}[\text{index}]), \ H_{3_c}(\text{«2»}, s_{1_{bc}}[\text{index}]))))\Big)$$

14.5.6 – Note the usages of H_{3_c} and H_{2_c}.

14.5.7 – In our third state, we clean up the result:

$$s_{2_{bc}} = \sigma_{bc}([\,], [\,], [\cdot], \text{«any-num»})$$

$$R(s_{2_{bc}}) \to \sigma_{bc}\Big([\,], [\,], [\,], s_{2_{bc}}[\text{value}]\Big)$$

14.5.8 – Finally, our machine specifier:

$$\mathcal{M}_{bc}(d, l) \equiv \sigma_{bc}(d, l, [\,], [\,])$$

14.5.9 – Let's look at an example, $\mathcal{M}_{bc}(\langle \text{«1»}, \text{«0»}, \text{«1»}\rangle, \text{«3»})$:

	«digits»	«length»	«index»	«value»
$\mathcal{M}_{bc}(\langle\text{«1»},\text{«0»},\text{«1»}\rangle,\text{«3»})$	$\langle\text{«1»},\text{«0»},\text{«1»}\rangle$	«3»	[ ]	[ ]
$R(s_{0_{bc}}) \to R(s_{1_{bc}})$	$\langle\text{«1»},\text{«0»},\text{«1»}\rangle$	«3»	«2»	«0»
$R(s_{1_{bc}}) \to R(s_{1_{bc}})$	$\langle\text{«1»},\text{«0»},\text{«1»}\rangle$	«3»	«2»	«4»
$R(s_{1_{bc}}) \to R(s_{1_{bc}})$	$\langle\text{«1»},\text{«0»},\text{«1»}\rangle$	«3»	«1»	«4»
$R(s_{1_{bc}}) \to R(s_{1_{bc}})$	$\langle\text{«1»},\text{«0»},\text{«1»}\rangle$	«3»	«0»	«5»
$R(s_{1_{bc}}) \to R(s_{2_{bc}})$	$\langle\text{«1»},\text{«0»},\text{«1»}\rangle$	«3»	[ ]	«5»
$R(s_{2_{bc}})$	[ ]	[ ]	[ ]	«5»

15 Decimal Machines

"Mathematics is the language with which God has written the universe."

— Galileo Galilei

It would seem imprudent to leave out our most common form of numeric representation: decimal numbers.

15.1 Decimal Numbers

15.1.1 – Decimal representations will largely resemble our binary scheme.

15.1.2 – In fact, our state specifier will be nearly identical to σ_b, defined in §14.1.2:

$$\sigma_d(s, v, c, i, d) \equiv$$

$$\Big\langle \langle \text{«state»}, s \rangle, \langle \text{«value»}, v \rangle, \langle \text{«current»}, c \rangle, \langle \text{«index»}, i \rangle, \langle \text{«digits»}, d \rangle \Big\rangle$$

15.1.3 – Our first state initiates our conversion:

$$s_{0_d} = \sigma_d\Big(\text{«begin»}, \; [\,], \; [\,], \; [\,], \; [\,] \Big)$$

$$R(s_{0_d}) \to \sigma_d\Big(\text{«iter»}, \; s_{0_d}[\text{value}], \; \text{«0»}, \; \text{«0»}, \; \langle \, \rangle \Big)$$

15.1.4 – s_{1_d} will represent the «iter» state in which «current» = «9». In this circumstance, set the «current» value to «0», increment «index», and set the state to «carry».

$$s_{1_d} = \sigma_d\Big(\text{«iter»}, \; \text{«not-0»}, \; \text{«9»}, \; [\,], \; [\,] \Big)$$

$$R(s_{1_d}) \to \sigma_d\Big(\text{«carry»}, \; s_{1_d}[\text{value}], \; s_{1_d}[\text{digits}][H_0(s_{1_d}[\text{index}])],$$

$$H_0(s_{1_d}[\text{index}]), \; T(s_{1_d}[\text{digits}], s_{1_d}[\text{index}], \text{«0»}) \Big)$$

15.1.5 – s_{2_d} will represent the «iter» state in which «current» < «9». This can be represented with «any-num», since «9» will match s_{1_d}. In this circumstance, we only increment the «current» value, referenced by «index» in «digits».

$$s_{2_d} = \sigma_d\Big(\text{«iter»}, \; \text{«not-0»}, \; \text{«any-num»}, \; [\,], \; [\,] \Big)$$

$$R(s_{2_d}) \to \sigma_d\Big(\text{«iter»}, \; H_0^{-1}(s_{2_d}[\text{value}]), \; H_0(s_{2_d}[\text{current}]),$$

$$s_{2_d}[\text{index}], \; T(s_{2_d}[\text{digits}], s_{2_d}[\text{index}], H_0(s_{2_d}[\text{current}])) \Big)$$

15.1.6 – s_{3_d} will represent the «carry» state in which the «current» digit is «9». In this circumstance, we set the «current» value to «0», referenced by «index» in «digits», and increment «index» (and repeat until «current» < «9»).

$$s_{3_d} = \sigma_d\Big(\text{«carry»},\ \text{«not-0»},\ \text{«\.{9}»},\ [\ ],\ [\ ]\Big)$$

$$R(s_{3_d}) \to \sigma_d\Big(\text{«carry»},\ s_{3_d}[\text{value}],\ s_{3_d}[\text{digits}][H_0(s_{3_d}[\text{index}])],$$
$$H_0(s_{3_d}[\text{index}]),\ T(s_{3_d}[\text{digits}],\ s_{3_d}[\text{index}],\ \text{«0»}),\Big)$$

15.1.7 – s_{4_d} will represent the «carry» state in which the «current» digit is less than «9». In this circumstance, we increment the «current» value, and reset «state» to «iter» and «index» to «0».

$$s_{4_d} = \sigma_b\Big(\text{«carry»},\ \text{«not-0»},\ \text{«any-num»},\ [\ ],\ [\ ]\Big)$$

$$R(s_{4_d}) \to \sigma_b\Big(\text{«iter»},\ H_0^{-1}(s_{4_d}[\text{value}]),\ s_{4_d}[\text{digits}][\text{«0»}],$$
$$\text{«0»},\ T(s_{4_d}[\text{digits}],\ s_{4_d}[\text{index}],\ H_0(s_{4_d}[\text{digits}][\text{index}]))\Big)$$

15.1.8 – This returns the machine to the state representation by s_{1_d} and continues adding each digit, until «value» is decreased to «0», exactly the same as $\mathcal{M}_b$.

15.1.9 – We «end» with our final value in [digits].

$$s_{5_d} = \sigma_d\Big(\text{«iter»},\ \text{«\.{0}»},\ [\ ],\ [\ ],\ [\ ]\Big)$$

$$R(s_{5_d}) \to \sigma_d\Big(\text{«end»},\ [\ ],\ [\ ],\ [\ ],\ s_{5_d}[\text{digits}]\Big)$$

15.1.10 – And here is our machine specifier:

$$\mathcal{M}_d(n) \equiv \sigma_d(\text{«begin»}, n, [\ ], [\ ], [\ ])$$

15.2 Example

15.2.1 – Let's show our conversion of «17» as an example:

	«state»	«value»	«current»	«index»	«digits»
$\mathcal{M}_d(\text{«17»})$	«begin»	«17»	[ ]	[ ]	[ ]
$R(s_{0_d}) \to s_{2_d}$	«iter»	«17»	«0»	«0»	$\langle\,\rangle$
$R(s_{2_d}) \to s_{2_d}$	«iter»	«16»	«1»	«0»	$\langle\text{«1»}\rangle$
$R(s_{2_d}) \to s_{2_d}$	«iter»	«15»	«2»	«0»	$\langle\text{«2»}\rangle$
$R(s_{2_d}) \to s_{2_d}$	«iter»	«14»	«3»	«0»	$\langle\text{«3»}\rangle$
$R(s_{2_d}) \to s_{2_d}$	«iter»	«13»	«4»	«0»	$\langle\text{«4»}\rangle$
$R(s_{2_d}) \to s_{2_d}$	«iter»	«12»	«5»	«0»	$\langle\text{«5»}\rangle$
$R(s_{2_d}) \to s_{2_d}$	«iter»	«11»	«6»	«0»	$\langle\text{«6»}\rangle$
$R(s_{2_d}) \to s_{2_d}$	«iter»	«10»	«7»	«0»	$\langle\text{«7»}\rangle$
$R(s_{2_d}) \to s_{2_d}$	«iter»	«9»	«8»	«0»	$\langle\text{«8»}\rangle$
$R(s_{2_d}) \to s_{1_d}$	«iter»	«8»	«9»	«0»	$\langle\text{«9»}\rangle$
$R(s_{1_d}) \to s_{4_d}$	«carry»	«8»	«0»	«1»	$\langle\text{«0»}\rangle$
$R(s_{4_d}) \to s_{2_d}$	«iter»	«7»	«0»	«0»	$\langle\text{«1»}, \text{«0»}\rangle$
$R(s_{2_d}) \to s_{2_d}$	«iter»	«6»	«1»	«0»	$\langle\text{«1»}, \text{«1»}\rangle$
$R(s_{2_d}) \to s_{2_d}$	«iter»	«5»	«2»	«0»	$\langle\text{«1»}, \text{«2»}\rangle$
$R(s_{2_d}) \to s_{2_d}$	«iter»	«4»	«3»	«0»	$\langle\text{«1»}, \text{«3»}\rangle$
$R(s_{2_d}) \to s_{2_d}$	«iter»	«3»	«4»	«0»	$\langle\text{«1»}, \text{«4»}\rangle$
$R(s_{2_d}) \to s_{2_d}$	«iter»	«2»	«5»	«0»	$\langle\text{«1»}, \text{«5»}\rangle$
$R(s_{2_d}) \to s_{2_d}$	«iter»	«1»	«6»	«0»	$\langle\text{«1»}, \text{«6»}\rangle$
$R(s_{2_d}) \to s_{2_d}$	«iter»	«0»	«7»	«0»	$\langle\text{«1»}, \text{«7»}\rangle$
$R(s_{2_d}) \to s_{5_d}$	«end»	[ ]	[ ]	[ ]	$\langle\text{«1»}, \text{«7»}\rangle$

15.2.2 – Following the example of the binary representations, it is possible to construct other operations in a similar manner.

16 Numerons

"The nervous system and the automatic machine are fundamentally alike in that they are devices, which make decisions on the basis of decisions they made in the past."

— Norbert Wiener

Though the term is used with different meanings, we will take the word *numeron* to indicate any representation of a quantity or magnitude in the mind or brain, from the level of molecules to complex conceptual machines.

16.1 Simple Representations of Quantity

16.1.1 – Recent experiments have indicated that even an individual neuron can learn some sense of quantity, in the form of predicting responses to intervals between two related stimuli.[15]

16.1.2 – This gives an indication that the smallest quantity-capable representations in the brain are sub-neural.

16.1.3 – It is an interesting exercise to think about the simplest possible forms of tracking and adapting to new intervals as physical automata.

16.2 Molecular Chains

16.2.1 – One extremely simple form of representation for the interval could be a simple chain of molecules. The exact type or form of these molecules is not important except that they can be chained together—and that a longer chain represents a longer interval (or quantity), while a shorter chain represents a short interval (or quantity).

16.2.2 – We can imagine some kind of molecular automaton that at any point in time holds itself to a specific point in the chain, representing its location within the interval.

16.2.3 – If the amount of time it takes the automaton to move from one link in the chain to another is roughly equal for each segment of the chain, the respective intervals between two chains of a similar length would also be roughly equal.

16.2.4 – So if we have molecular chains of the appropriate length available, the interval from the time that the automaton would begin traversing the chain to the time that the automaton would complete the chain would be roughly equivalent to the interval between the first and second phenomena.

16.2.5 – If the traversal process was triggered by the first phenomena, which we will call A, it would end at approximately the time of the second phenomena, phenomena B—which would allow it to trigger a response at near the same time as the second phenomena.

16.3 Learning Intervals

16.3.1 – This system of molecular chains and automata gives us a method of representing and delaying a reaction in roughly the same interval as some outside phenomena.

---

[15]See Johansson et al. (2014).

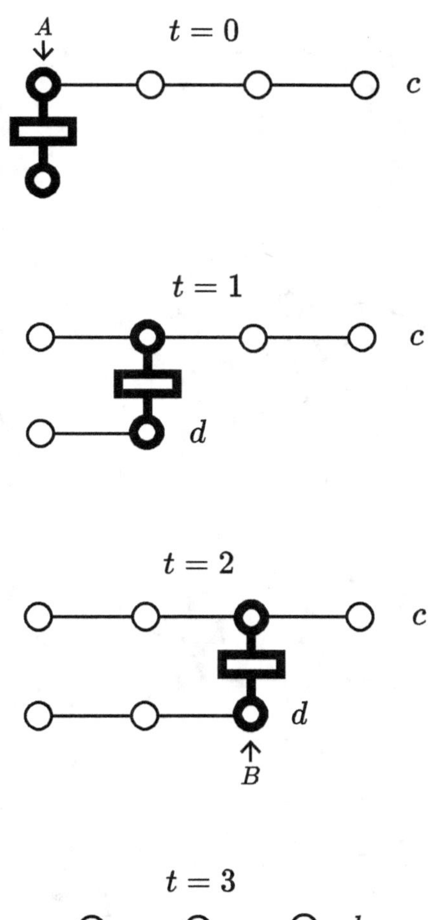

Figure 33: *Numeron Chain Shrinking:* When the interval between A and B is less than that indicated by chain c, the resulting chain d will be shorter. The next repetition, chain d will produce the action at the end of the interval more quickly than chain c did.

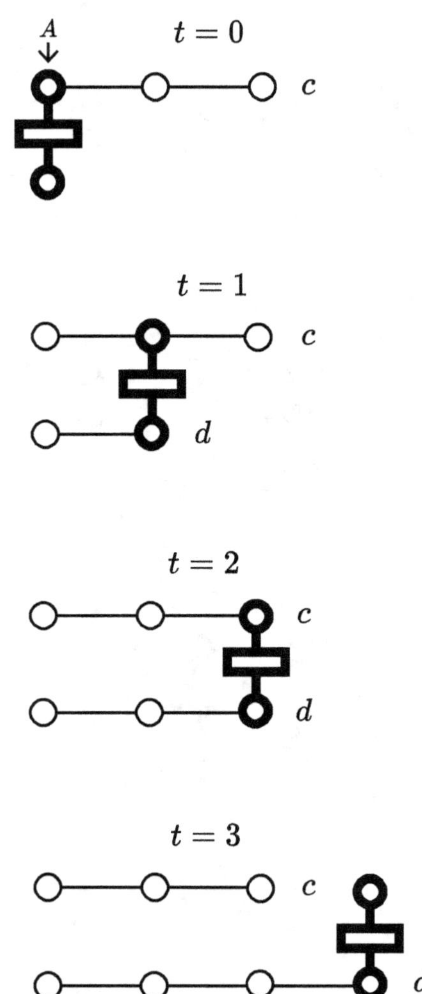

Figure 34: *Numeron Chain Growing:* In exact contrast to the previous scenario, when the interval between *A* and *B* is *greater* than that indicated by chain *c*, the resulting chain *d* will be *longer*. Chain *d* will produce the action at the end of the interval *less* quickly than chain *c* did.

16.3.2 – But we still need a way for the system to learn new intervals—again, trying to draw the simplest possible explanation.

16.3.3 – Let's imagine that the automaton not only begins traversing existing molecular chains when A occurs, but it will also begin constructing a new molecular chain, chain d at the same rate that it traverses an existing chain, which we will call chain c.

16.3.4 – If B occurs before chain c is traversed, the automaton halts the construction of the new chain d such that it is shorter than c—meaning that the next time when d is traversed, the interval will accordingly be shortened.

16.3.5 – If B occurs *after* chain c is traversed, the automaton will continue building the new chain d longer than c. Accordingly, the interval for processing d will be shorter than c.

16.3.6 – It would seem pretty simplistic to think that this is actually what is occurring in a cell. But one could imagine that there are thousands or more of these chains and automata, from which the stochastic element of when an automaton encounters a chain, etc., such a simple mechanism begins to seem more plausible.

16.4 Counting Numbers

16.4.1 – In our conceptual system, we represent counting numbers as discrete chains of composed concepts.

16.4.2 – This system does have many properties that make it plausible as an actual counting system.

16.4.3 – Without the aid of digital systems, counting can only occur either to the extent that subitization or some other direct representation can be made, or else by relating smaller quantities. In the second case, an example might be "okay there are twice as many of this amount as that amount," where *that amount* is four. Further, we could see the concept of *twice as many as that amount plus one*, etc. We can begin to see the seeds of a system evolving that represents larger quantities in terms of smaller quantities as in Roman numerals (instead of 30, there are three tens).

16.4.4 – These structures constitute simple conceptual mechanisms for conveying quantities.

16.5 Digital Numbers

16.5.1 – The digital number has the property of being indefinitely recursive, such that with a single, finite conceptual machine we can represent arbitrary quantities.

16.5.2 – The digital numbers we are most familiar with are of course decimal numbers, but there are alternate digital systems such as binary numbers.

16.5.3 – There are even extreme examples, such as the Babylonians, who used a base-60 system that had 60 different digits (and therefore 60 different concepts). But the idea is the same as binary or decimal.

16.5.4 – In a digital system, only a concept for each of the digits is required, along with a rule for changing the amount that is represented based on the digit's place in the number.

16.5.5 – In practice we likely have separate concepts that are independent of our digital representations for certain numbers we are more familiar with.

16.5.6 – For example, we may have a concept as «four» that has relations to «4_c», «4_b», «4_d», as well as certain patterns that we can subitize as four, the actual numeral "4," etc.

16.5.7 – Our mind puts those alternate representations to use based on the needs of a given scenario, sometimes in combination.

16.5.8 – For example, when we add, we are not usually following the exact rules of an addition machine like we've outlined in preceding chapters.

16.5.9 – For example, if you ask me to calculate $27 + 94$, I first know that the last digit will be «1» as a result of a pattern that applies to the specific digits «7» and «4» and that I will need to add «1» to the resulting tens digit of my calculation. Then I add «2» and «9» to get «11» (again pattern recognition completely due to the digits) add a «0» to the end because I know it's the tens place to get «110», add the carried «1» from the addition of «7» and «4» to the tens place to get «120», and finally place the last digit «1» into the result to get «121».

16.5.10 – Nonetheless, the decimal representation gives us a sense of what this quantity means outside of a counting context. I know «121» means 1 "hundred," 2 "tens," and 1.

16.5.11 – When I need to exploit my actual digital conceptual machines, I can—as when I mechanically add two much larger numbers together, say «938365832» and «735549631».

16.5.12 – These conceptual machines are not as reliable as ingrained pattern recognition, but it allows us to expand our numerical capacity beyond what it would otherwise be.

16.6 Intuitive Numbers

16.6.1 – I suspect that most of us have a type of numerical representation that I call an *intuitive number* that we use for estimating and working with general quantities.

16.6.2 – The information contained in an intuitive number is a different for each person, but let me illustrate the type of structure I'm talking about first.

$$\nu_i(s, d, f_n, f_d, o_m) = \Big\langle \langle \text{«sign»}, s\rangle, \ \langle \text{«decimal»}, d\rangle, \ \langle \text{«numerator»}, f_n\rangle,$$
$$\langle \text{«denominator»}, f_d\rangle, \ \langle \text{«magnitude»}, o_m\rangle \Big\rangle$$

16.6.3 – This type of representation can represent a sign (i.e. «positive» or «negative»), a decimal representation of the whole number, a representation of the «numerator» and «denominator» of the fractional part—both also decimal numbers—and a «magnitude».

16.6.4 – The «magnitude» ties the other portions of the representation back to *what* it is representing. A magnitude can either be some other numeric representation—such as «thousands» or «tens»—or it can be a more concrete magnitude, such as «apples».

16.6.5 – In this way, when a numeric «magnitude» is used, it makes our intuitive numbers function much like scientific numbers.

16.6.6 – And there might be further representations that vary person to person. So if someone works frequently with complex numbers, there may be an additional «imaginary» component, for example.

17 Language

"Since language is clearly a computational system, the relevant laws of nature should include (and perhaps be limited to) principles of efficient computation."

— Noam Chomsky

Nearly inseparable, language is the most critical capability to understand our conceptual faculties. We now take a closer examination of how the human system of symbolic conceptualization operates through language.

17.1 Grammar & Relationships

17.1.1 – The human language faculty maps our conceptual system onto some form of symbolic encoding, and turns complex conceptual relationships into simpler contextual, hierarchical, or order-based relationships.

17.1.2 – The rules for how symbols in a language are combined are called its *grammar*.

17.1.3 – The exact nature of the combinations determines what relationships the concepts represented by each symbol hold with each other.

17.1.4 – Languages are tools for manipulating and representing relationships between concepts, along with conceptual machines for transforming conceptual structures to and from symbolic representations.

17.1.5 – We will call the conceptual machine that takes a conceptual structure and turns it into a linguistic representation $\mathcal{M}_S$.

17.1.6 – Although the mechanical structure of $\mathcal{M}_S$ is far too complex to explore in this book, we can show its operation by way of an example, with some further linguistic structure than we've shown to this point:

$$\text{«draw»} = \langle [\text{artist}],\ [\text{subject}], \dots \rangle$$

$$s = \Big\langle \langle \text{«artist»}, \text{«Bob»}\rangle,\ \langle \text{«tense»}, \text{«past-tense»}\rangle,$$

$$\langle \text{«subject»}, \langle \text{«Mona Lisa»}, \text{«definite article»}\rangle\rangle, \dots \Big\rangle$$

$$R(\mathcal{M}_S(s)) \to \text{«Bob drew the Mona Lisa»}$$

17.1.7 – We can define operation S, *symbolize* to enact this machine:

$$S(a) \equiv R(\mathcal{M}_S(a))$$

17.1.8 – We also can imagine an inverse machine $\mathcal{M}_S^{-1}$ which takes a concept of a linguistic expression and retrieves its conceptual structure.

17.1.9 – $\mathcal{M}_S^{-1}$, also shown by example:

$$R(\mathcal{M}_S^{-1}(\text{«Bob drew the Mona Lisa»})) \to s$$

17.1.10 – And its operation S^{-1}:

$$S^{-1}(a) \equiv R(\mathcal{M}_S^{-1}(a))$$

17.2 Human Language

17.2.1 – The most common symbolic system used in human beings is speech. But others, such as writing and sign language, are also common.

17.2.2 – When the speech system of symbolization is available (i.e. to those who are not born deaf), it takes primacy.

17.2.3 – When we read, we "hear" the words in our head.

17.2.4 – We cannot read without "hearing" also. Try reading this sentence without "saying the words" to yourself also.

17.2.5 – We sometimes modulate our breathing patterns or even manipulate our larynx as if we were speaking the words ourselves. We can almost "feel" ourselves speaking.

17.2.6 – Below we illustrate the general process using our operations defined previously. The writing evokes "sounds" of the words in our mind. The sounds are further interpreted to their associated concepts, and by *recountation* can give the sensation of speaking.

$$I(\{\text{‹writing›}\}) \rightarrow \text{«sound»}$$

$$S^{-1}(\text{«sound»}) \rightarrow a$$

$$R(\text{«sound»}) \rightarrow \text{«sensation of speaking»}$$

17.2.7 – This primacy of spoken forms of language is not surprising, because human beings seem to use spoken language in their natural environment.

17.2.8 – What is more surprising is the ease with which other modes of symbolization are adapted.

17.3 Language & Conceptualization

17.3.1 – Many of the most-developed countries in the world approach a 100% literacy rate.[16] But how can this be?

17.3.2 – Writing is only a few thousand years old, and it developed several times independently.[17] Our species did not have time for natural selection to select for reading ability.

17.3.3 – Groups of deaf children have also been observed to invent ad hoc sign languages nearly immediately when none was available to be taught to them.[18]

---

[16]Roser & Ortiz-Ospina (2013).
[17]Clayton (2019).
[18]Senghas & Coppola (2001).

17.3.4 – These facts gives us a hint as to what language *is*. Language is a system for mapping concepts into a system of symbolization.

17.3.5 – The form of symbolization has a grammar—a system of ordering or other attributes that produce a hierarchical conceptual structure—and a vocabulary—a set of words that map to concepts.

17.3.6 – There are two systems that are distinct but intertwined—the system of *concepts* and their relations to form structures and mechanisms—and the linguistic system of vocabulary and grammar, which determines the representation of those concepts in the symbolic form.[19]

17.3.7 – The system of vocabulary and grammar vary depending on the specific language in use. But the general conceptual system is almost entirely the same. Although the structure and vocabulary of a language can shape and limit what we say to some extent, most natural languages give wide latitude to express nearly equivalent concepts.[20]

17.3.8 – Being deaf can alter the human brain much more significantly than being blind. In deaf people, if they are taught to sign early, there is no significant difference in cognitive abilities in comparison to the general population. But if a young deaf child is not taught to sign, either because it is not discovered that they are deaf or because sign education is not available to them, nearly every cognitive aspect of the mind is dampened.[21]

17.3.9 – This shows that our symbolization faculty operates as a catalyst for the conceptual system.

17.3.10 – We can understand why this is. When given a system for symbolization, we gain the ability to quickly tag a label onto a concept and then manipulate it without holding all details of the concept in our working memory.

17.3.11 – Concepts allow for perceptions to be recalled for manipulation; language allows for concepts to be recalled and manipulated in the same way.

17.3.12 – For example, to a chess master, you only need to tell them to picture "the Philador position." To a less-experienced player you will need to explain, "black's king is on f4, his pawn is on e4," etc. There will be several pieces of information they have to hold in their head, while the master just recalls «the Philador position».[22]

17.3.13 – The master can then extend this trick outside the Philador position, by thinking things like "the Philador position, but the king is on f5."

---

[19]Dufour & Kroll (1995).
[20]Ibid.
[21]Hall (2017).
[22]Howell (1997).

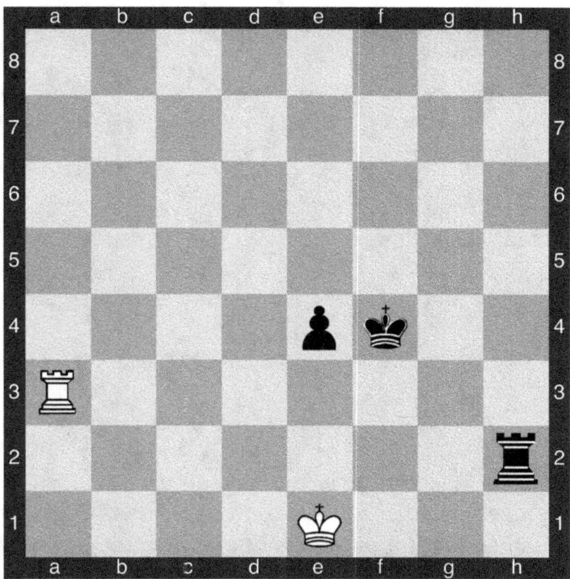

Figure 35: *Philador Position:* The Philador position is an endgame position well-known in chess theory.

17.3.14 – The chess master has a concept, «the Philador position», that the novice doesn't possess. And he has a convenient label, the words "Philador position" to express it in.

17.3.15 – Words themselves *may* be components of a concept, and are *always* relations to their concepts.

17.3.16 – Multilingual patients with Alzheimer's tend to retain higher levels of cognition that those who don't.[23] This is presumably because as certain relations between concepts are severed, say between the concept «chair» and the concept of the English word "chair," others are still intact, such as the connection between the concept «chair» and the Spanish word "silla."[24]

17.3.17 – When deaf people "think to themselves," they do similar things to what a non-deaf person does, but in their own mode of symbolism. They "feel" their hands signing, as we can almost "feel" ourselves speaking. They can "see" the signs, as we can almost hear the words.[25]

$$I(\{\langle\text{sign}\rangle\}) \to \text{«sign»}$$

$$R(\text{«sign»}) \to \text{«sensation of signing»}$$

---

[23]Duncan et al. (2018).
[24]Dufour & Kroll (1995).
[25]Klima & Bellugi (1979).

17.4 Language & Perception

17.4.1 – When we hear speech (or see signs or written words), we immediately jump to the concepts and nearly immediately discard the primitive perceptual and sensory data.

17.4.2 – If you see the word "green" in a yellow tone, you will first think "green" before thinking yellow, even when you are specifically prompted to try to say the color.[26]

$$I(\{\text{"green"}, \langle\text{yellow}\rangle\}) \to \text{«green»}$$

17.4.3 – When you hear a person speaking in another language, you will notice the oddities of the sounds *as sounds*. But if you try to listen to your own native language as a series of sounds you will be flooded with a stream of concepts and thoughts about subtle linguistic cues given by the speaker, with almost no ability to isolate the sounds on their own merit.

17.4.4 – Our language faculty is so inveterate in us that it almost takes the place of one of our primary perceptions, and at the very minimum alters our sensory perceptions significantly.

17.5 Communication

17.5.1 – Communication is the replication of a conceptual structure from one mind to another, most often via language.

17.5.2 – Let's illustrate an exchange between two persons A and B.

$$c_A = \Big\langle \langle\text{«subject»}, \text{«I»}\rangle, \ \langle\text{«attribute»}, \text{«hungry»}\rangle, \ \dots \Big\rangle$$

$$c_B = \Big\langle \langle\text{«subject»}, \text{«they»}\rangle, \ \langle\text{«attribute»}, \text{«hungry»}\rangle, \ \dots \Big\rangle$$

$$S_A(c_A) \to \text{"I am hungry"}$$

$$I_B(\{\text{"I am hungry"}\}) \to \text{«I am hungry»}$$

$$S_B^{-1}(\text{«I am hungry»}) \to c_A$$

$$R_B(c_A) \to c_B$$

---

[26]This is known as the *Stroop effect*, see Stroop (1935).

17.6 Internal Language

17.6.1 – Language is, as much as it is for communication, a system for recalling and manipulating concepts to hold new relationships to each other.

17.6.2 – Our minds use language as a tool to make our ability to manipulate concepts more efficient. This is our *internal language.*

17.6.3 – We all experience inner conceptualization, most often accompanied by symbols that we enact only in our minds, such as imaginary self-speech.

17.6.4 – We "speak" much more often to ourselves, usually many times more, than to others.[27]

17.6.5 – This is a strong indication that the purposes of language are as much conceptual (i.e. internal to the mind) as they are communicative (external to the mind).

17.7 Language Ambiguity

17.7.1 – Certain uses of language are ambiguous and can map to more than one interpretation.

17.7.2 – This is exactly what we would expect if the mind's conceptual system is related to—but separate from—its symbolic system.

17.7.3 – Take the statement *Mary saw Bob walking to the park.* This statement has three interpretations, each with a different meaning (or conceptual structure).[28]

17.7.4 – The first is equivalent to: "Mary saw Bob *as he was walking* to the park." The second is equivalent to: "Mary saw Bob *as she was walking* to the park." The final interpretation, similar but subtly different from the first is: "Mary saw *Bob's act of walking* to the park."

17.7.5 – Importantly, the statement can have all three meanings with the exact same intonation.

17.7.6 – We can cycle through each interpretation of the sentence in our minds, but can only hold one meaning to our attention at once.

17.7.7 – This shows us that the conceptual structure that lies beneath language is independent of the grammatical structure of language.

---

[27]See Morin, Uttl & Hamper (2011). They found that approximately 20% of our inner experience was inner speech, vastly outweighing even liberal estimates of how often we converse with others.

[28]This is similar to an example given by Chomsky.

18 Computation

"[O]n the basis of what has been proved so far, it remains possible that there may exist (and even be empirically discoverable) a theorem proving machine which in fact is equivalent to mathematical intuition, but cannot be proved to be so, nor even be proved to yield only correct theorems of finitary number theory."

— Kurt Gödel

In this chapter, we will show that our framework can be used to emulate a Turing machine, demonstrating its computational completeness.

18.1 Turing Machines

18.1.1 – A Turing machine is a hypothetical machine invented by Alan Turing capable of emulating any possible computational process.[29]

18.1.2 – By demonstrating that our mechanical framework can emulate any Turing machine, we will demonstrate that our framework is *Turing-complete*, i.e. that it also can perform any possible computation.

18.1.3 – A Turing machine has two main components.

18.1.4 – The first is a tape, divided into a number of squares. At any point in time there is a pointer, called the head, that points to exactly one of those squares.

18.1.5 – The second component is a set of configuration rules. Each rule specifies that when the machine is in a given state, some transformation in the state should occur.

18.1.6 – Each machine state is indicated generally by a short label, which may consist of one or more Gothic letters. By convention the first machine state is indicated $\mathfrak{b}$.

18.1.7 – The combination of this configuration label and the symbol the head is pointing to determine which configuration rule to follow.

18.1.8 – The configuration rule can then indicate whether a new symbol should be written in the square indicated by the current head, whether the final operation should result in moving the head right or left one or more squares, and the final configuration label, which will serve as the marker for the next configuration state to follow.

18.1.9 – By convention, alternating squares mark out digits of the final result, with the spaces in between reserved for marking each digit for purposes of calculation.

18.1.10 – Also by convention, traditional Turing machines compute binary numbers, and do not overwrite result digits after they've been written.

18.1.11 – A traditional Turing machine is valid only if it is "circle-free," i.e. if it will continue writing digits indefinitely without halting.

18.1.12 – Each configuration rule is indicated in a table format.

18.1.13 – We will demonstrate with the first example from Turing's original 1936 paper:

---

[29]Turing (1936)

config	symbol	operations	final config
b	None	$P0, R$	c
c	None	R	e
e	None	$P1, R$	f
f	None	R	b

18.1.14 – Let's see what this does. First, we begin in configuration b and our head at the beginning of a blank tape.

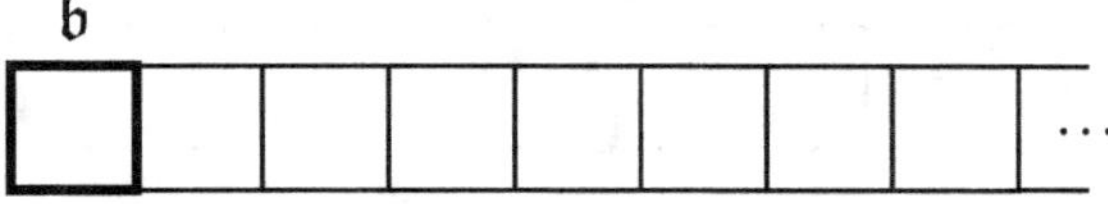

Figure 36: *Turing Machine State* b

18.1.15 – The "None," indicates that this configuration applies if there is no symbol in the square pointed to by the head. Under *operations*, $P0, R$ indicates that we should write (or *put*) the symbol "0," then move to the right.

18.1.16 – Here is our current tape:

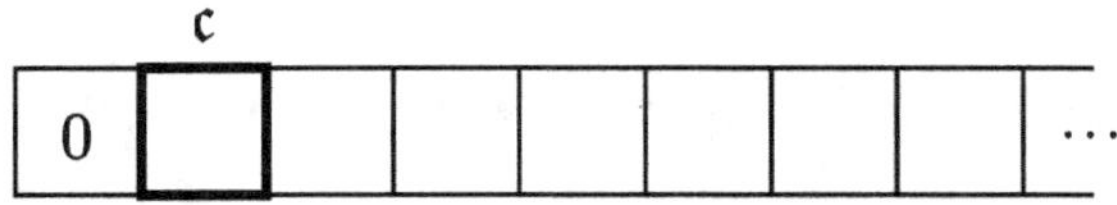

Figure 37: *Turing Machine State* c

18.1.17 – After the operation is performed, it indicated that our *final config* is to be c. So we next refer to the rules that pertain to config c.

18.1.18 – c indicates that we should move right one more square, following the conventional style to skip squares between our digits:

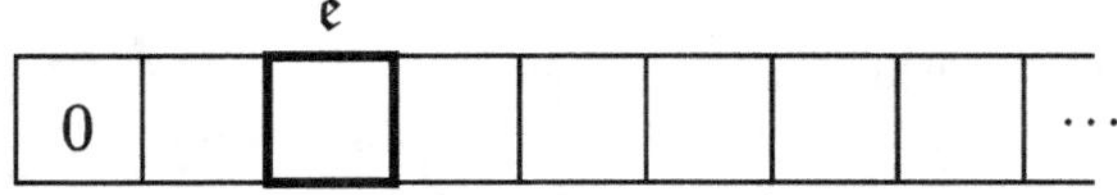

Figure 38: *Turing Machine State* e

18.1.19 – We then switch to $\mathfrak{e}$ which indicates that we should put a "1" and move to the right:

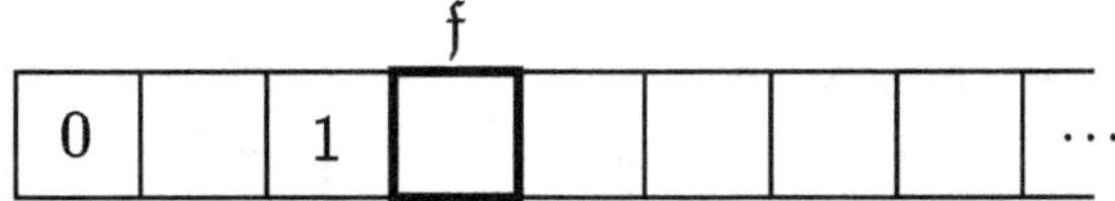

Figure 39: *Turing Machine State* $\mathfrak{f}$

18.1.20 – And then $\mathfrak{f}$ which indicates that we should move to the right again and go back to state $\mathfrak{b}$:

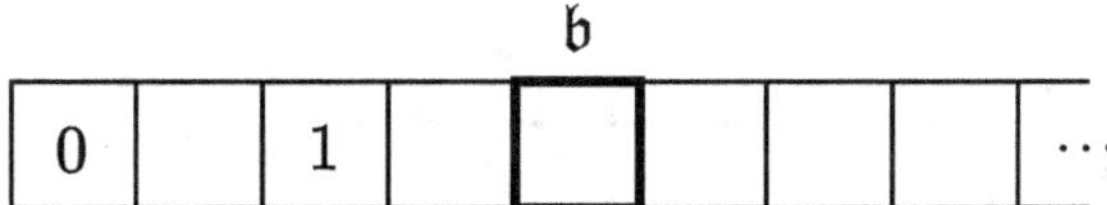

Figure 40: *Turing Machine State* $\mathfrak{b}$

18.1.21 – And from there the cycle repeats:

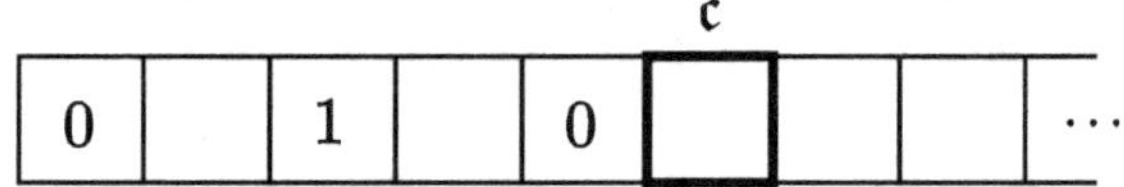

Figure 41: *Turing Machine State* $\mathfrak{c}$

18.1.22 – The machine will continue to write alternating 0's and 1's in perpetuity.

18.1.23 – It should be noted that this sequence represents the number $\frac{1}{3}$ (in binary: 0.01010101 ...). All numbers in the sequence are assumed to appear after the "binary decimal" point.

18.1.24 – For further examples, you can refer back to the original paper, or to the many of studies on Turing machines that have been published since.

18.2 Universality

18.2.1 – One key feature of Turing machines is that Alan Turing showed in his paper that a *universal* Turing machine can be built: a Turing machine that can emulate any other Turing machine.[30]

---

[30]Turing (1936).

18.2.2 – Its full set of configuration rules are given in the paper, so we will omit them here. But this fact allows for a universal Turing machine to perform any possible computation.[31] This is known as the Church-Turing thesis.

18.2.3 – Similarly, any system that can emulate any Turing machine can therefore also be used to perform any possible computation.

18.2.4 – We will now show that our system can emulate a Turing machine, specifically the example above.

18.3 Emulation

18.3.1 – In order to emulate the Turing machine above, we first have to determine how each part of the Turing machine will be represented in our framework.

18.3.2 – Let's start with a conceptual structure that will hold the full current state of the tape as a «sequence», the index of the cell that is currently being pointed to by the head as its «index», and the symbol currently on the tape at the «index» position as «current». «sequence» will function as a typical «sequence», but it will yield [ ] for empty «index»'s instead of «0».

18.3.3 – Here's our machine specifier:

$$\sigma_T(s,q,i,c) = \Big\langle \langle\text{«state»}, s\rangle,\ \langle\text{«current»}, c\rangle,\ \langle\text{«sequence»}, q\rangle,\ \langle\text{«index»}, i\rangle \Big\rangle$$

$$: \Upsilon(\{\text{«b»}, \text{«c»}, \text{«e»}, \text{«f»}\}, \text{«state»})$$

18.3.4 – Now we can define each of the configuration rules as relations between states. Our first state will emulate configuration $\mathfrak{b}$:

$$s_\mathfrak{b} = \sigma_T(\text{«b»}, [\cdot], [\,], [\,])$$

$$R(s_\mathfrak{b}) \rightarrow \sigma_T\Big(\text{«c»},\ X(s_\mathfrak{b}[\text{sequence}], H_0(s_\mathfrak{b}[\text{index}])),$$

$$T(s_\mathfrak{b}[\text{sequence}], s_\mathfrak{b}[\text{index}], \text{«0»}),\ H_0(s_\mathfrak{b}[\text{index}])\Big)$$

18.3.5 – Let's examine each part of this rule to see how it matches to configuration $\mathfrak{b}$ in the Turing machine above.

18.3.6 – The first item of note is that the first two columns in the table match to the first two fields is $s_\mathfrak{b}$. «b» indicates the configuration rule $\mathfrak{b}$, and [·] matches a literal proxy, an empty sequence item.

---

[31]Ibid.

18.3.7 – In the relation, we can see that the resulting «state» is «c», i.e. configuration state $\mathfrak{c}$.

18.3.8 – We also note that «current» is set to extract the «sequence» item that follows the current «index», incrementing it with operation H_0. This is due to the head moving right. If the head were to move to the left, it would instead utilize H_0^{-1} to decrement «index» and use that value instead.

18.3.9 – If there were no move operation for this configuration, «current» would simply be the symbol we write to the current square.

18.3.10 – The operation $T(s_\mathfrak{b}[\text{sequence}], s_\mathfrak{b}[\text{index}], «0»)$, writes the symbol «0» to the current «index».

18.3.11 – Finally, we use $H_0(s_\mathfrak{b}[\text{index}])$ to increment the current index, the equivalent of moving the head one square to the right.

18.3.12 – Similarly to how we gathered the next value of «current», this operation may use H_0^{-1} to move to the left, or will simply recall $s_\mathfrak{b}[\text{index}]$ if no movement is required.

18.3.13 – We use the same principles to define operations $\mathfrak{c}$, $\mathfrak{e}$, and $\mathfrak{f}$.

18.3.14 – $s_\mathfrak{c}$ simply moves the head one cell to the right and sets the state to «e»:

$$s_\mathfrak{c} = \sigma_T(«c», [\cdot], [\,], [\,])$$

$$R(s_\mathfrak{c}) \to \sigma_T\Big(«e», \; X(s_\mathfrak{c}[\text{sequence}], H_0(s_\mathfrak{c}[\text{index}])),$$
$$s_\mathfrak{c}[\text{sequence}], \; H_0(s_\mathfrak{c}[\text{index}]) \Big)$$

18.3.15 – $s_\mathfrak{e}$ writes «1», moves one cell to the right, and set the state to «f»:

$$s_\mathfrak{e} = \sigma_T(«e», [\cdot], [\,], [\,])$$

$$R(s_\mathfrak{e}) \to \sigma_T\Big(«f», \; X(s_\mathfrak{e}[\text{sequence}], H_0(s_\mathfrak{e}[\text{index}])),$$
$$T(s_\mathfrak{e}[\text{sequence}], s_\mathfrak{e}[\text{index}], «1»), \; H_0(s_\mathfrak{e}[\text{index}]) \Big)$$

18.3.16 – And $s_\mathfrak{f}$ moves one cell to the right and set the state to «b», renewing the cycle:

$$s_\mathfrak{f} = \sigma_T(«f», [\cdot], [\,], [\,])$$

$$R(s_\mathfrak{f}) \to \sigma_T\Big(«b», \; X(s_\mathfrak{f}[\text{sequence}], H_0(s_\mathfrak{f}[\text{index}])),$$
$$s_\mathfrak{f}[\text{sequence}], \; H_0(s_\mathfrak{f}[\text{index}]) \Big)$$

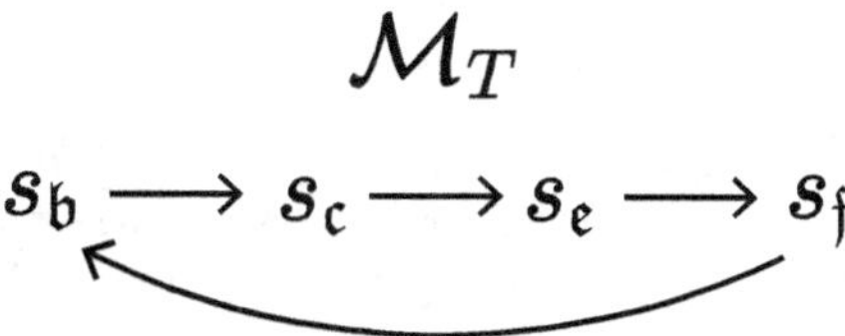

Figure 42: *Turing Machine State Graph*: Notice that, because it represents a well-formed Turing machine, this graph never terminates.

18.3.17 – Here's our execution table:

	«state»	«current»	«sequence»	«index»
s_b	«b»	[ ]	$\langle\rangle$	«$\bar{0}$»
$R(s_b) \to s_c$	«c»	[ ]	$\langle\text{«0»}\rangle$	«$\bar{1}$»
$R(s_c) \to s_e$	«e»	[ ]	$\langle\text{«0»},[\,]\rangle$	«$\bar{2}$»
$R(s_e) \to s_f$	«f»	[ ]	$\langle\text{«0»},[\,],\text{«1»}\rangle$	«$\bar{3}$»
$R(s_f) \to s_b$	«b»	[ ]	$\langle\text{«0»},[\,],\text{«1»},[\,]\rangle$	«$\bar{4}$»
$R(s_b) \to s_c$	«c»	[ ]	$\langle\text{«0»},[\,],\text{«1»},[\,],\text{«0»}\rangle$	«$\bar{5}$»
$R(s_c) \to s_e$	«e»	[ ]	$\langle\text{«0»},[\,],\text{«1»},[\,],\text{«0»},[\,]\rangle$	«$\bar{6}$»
$R(s_e) \to s_f$	«f»	[ ]	$\langle\text{«0»},[\,],\text{«1»},[\,],\text{«0»},[\,],\text{«1»}\rangle$	«$\bar{7}$»
$R(s_f) \to s_b$	«b»	[ ]	$\langle\text{«0»},[\,],\text{«1»},[\,],\text{«0»},[\,],\text{«1»},[\,]\rangle$	«$\bar{8}$»

18.3.18 – This demonstration shows that our mechanical framework can emulate every functional structure and operation of any Turing machine.

18.3.19 – These include:

1. The tape, via «sequence»;
2. The head, via «current» and «index»;
3. Configuration rules, including restrictions on which apply using «state» and «current», via relations;
4. Turing machine operation *put*, P, via T acting on «sequence»;
5. Turing machine operation *right*, R, via H_0 acting on «index»; and
6. Turing machine operation *left*, L, via H_0^{-1} acting on «index».

18.3.20 – Therefore, any system that can be specified as a Turing machine has an equivalent conceptual machine.

18.4 Significance

18.4.1 – It would be fair to ask: *What is the significance of the system's Turing-completeness?* We now know of a vast array of Turing-complete systems. What make this one of any particular interest?

18.4.2 – To start, it is of some level of interest that the primitives of the system have been specifically motivated by simple cognitive capabilities, with highly plausible inferences made to reach them.

18.4.3 – Second, the elementary constituents of a computational system very much matter in practice. If we were to build a discrete program search of Turing machines to perform exponentiation, say, that Turing machine would be much more complex than the exponentiation machine we've defined in the course of this book.[32]

18.4.4 – Finally, the system's Turing-complete nature allows us to do something very interesting: to build a conceptual machine that can emulate any other conceptual machine.

---

[32]This subject is of particular interest to me and is something I plan to explore in future work.

19 Universal Machines

"It is possible to invent a single machine which can be used to compute any computable sequence."

— Alan Turing

A conceptual machine can be built such that it can emulate any other conceptual machine—a *universal conceptual machine.*

19.1 Universal Conceptual Machine

19.1.1 – We can now draw influence from the universal Turing machine to develop our own machine that is capable of emulating any other conceptual machine—a *universal conceptual machine*.

19.1.2 – Though we will outline the construction of one such machine, $\mathcal{M}_U$, there are other possible ways of constructing equivalent machines.

19.1.3 – The machine will be constructed such that the behavior of the machine is specified entirely by its initial state, without any need for new relations to be defined in order to emulate any other conceptual machine.

19.1.4 – This gives us the ability to define and store the behavior of arbitrary machines in an entirely structural manner, a potentially useful capability for a mind.

19.1.5 – We can imagine a mind that experiments by putting together different structures that can be fed into its universal machine. The mind could iterate over different structural and relational possibilities without developing the need for an entirely new relational procedure for each possibility.

19.1.6 – Though this general procedure would be more cumbersome, it would allow for exploration of possible approaches to novel problems, and would allow for the storing of idioms and paradigms that worked in previous conceptual machines for use in later machines.

19.1.7 – This would explain how we can learn new mental processes by analogy to previous structures that worked.

19.1.8 – It could also indicate why we are slow to learn some new cognitive processes at first, because they are laboriously being implemented in a type of universal conceptual machine.

19.1.9 – Once the process has been learned, the mind can convert the structure given to the universal machine into a new set of concept states and their relations, internalizing the process.

19.1.10 – The ability for the mind to create new, arbitrary conceptual machines *ad hoc* may be the defining aspect of human creativity.

19.2 Machine Structure

19.2.1 – Because the set of relations that must be defined to put the workings of the universal machine in place are somewhat complicated, we're going to take a slightly different approach in this chapter to defining our machine.

19.2.2 – First, we are going to define specifiers for the machine architecture and to represent each necessary operation. Then we are going to demonstrate the structure that will emulate our machine to add counting numbers $\mathcal{M}_{1_c}$ (defined in §13.2) *before* we give the relations that actually make the structure of the machine work.

19.2.3 – For this machine it is important to have an eye on the targeted structure we want to have in place to define emulated machines, which will hopefully elucidate the general direction we are headed as we work through the relations, which are a bit more ponderous than those we've outlined so far.

19.2.4 – To start, our machine specifier σ_U:

$$\sigma_U(s, c, i, n, m, j, r) \equiv \Big\langle \langle \text{«structure»}, s \rangle, \ \langle \text{«configurations»}, c \rangle, \ \langle \text{«index»}, i \rangle,$$
$$\langle \text{«next»}, n \rangle, \ \langle \text{«matched»}, m \rangle, \ \langle \text{«instruction»}, j \rangle, \ \langle \text{«result»}, r \rangle \Big\rangle$$

19.2.5 – «structure» is an arbitrary conceptual structure that represents the state of the machine we are emulating.

19.2.6 – «configurations» is a «sequence» of configurations that yield a proxy when no match is found via operation X'. Each configuration has the form specified by:

$$\sigma_{c_U}(p, i) \equiv \Big\langle \langle \text{«pattern»}, p \rangle, \ \langle \text{«instruction»}, i \rangle \Big\rangle$$

19.2.7 – A configuration represents a state and relation of the machine. «pattern» is an arbitrary conceptual structure that is compared to «structure» to determine if this configuration applies to the current state of the emulated machine. Each configuration is iterated through until one is found that matches the current structure. If so, «instruction» defines a set of operations that will be performed on «structure».

19.2.8 – We also have a shorthand for the above that denotes σ_{c_U} as an arrow with c_U under it:

$$\sigma_{c_U}(p, i) \equiv p \underset{c_U}{\to} i$$

19.2.9 – We will cover «instruction»'s further below.

19.2.10 – «index» is a «numeral» that indicates the current configuration in «configurations».

19.2.11 – «next» represents the next configuration to be applied. This is used to determine if there are no further instructions; if so the machine will halt.

19.2.12 – «matched» is the result of the operation Y, either «true» or «false» depending on whether «structure» matches the current pattern.

19.2.13 – «instruction» is the instruction from the matched configuration.

19.2.14 – When the machine is finished executing, the result of the operation—the final state of «structure»—will appear in «result».

19.2.15 – We can begin to see a rough sketch of how this machine will work, emulating the process that a conceptual machine would generally follow to execute by sequentially testing each configuration to see if its «pattern» matches the machine's «structure».

19.2.16 – But there is a critical component that we have yet to define: how the «instruction»'s are operations, represented as conceptual structures that will be applied to the machine's «structure».

19.2.17 – For convenience in defining new machines, we have the machine specifier $\mathcal{M}_U$:

$$\mathcal{M}_U(s,c) = \sigma_U(s, c, [\,], [\,], [\,], [\,], [\,])$$

19.2.18 – As well as a machine specifier to show the result of a machine:

$$\mathcal{M}_{U_r}(r) = \sigma_U([\,], [\,], [\,], [\,], [\,], [\,], r)$$

19.3 Operation Specifiers

19.3.1 – To define operations, we'll create new *operation specifiers* indicated by a subscript σ, after the operation name.

19.3.2 – For example $C_{2\sigma}$, which represents operation C with two components:

$$C_{2\sigma}(o_1, o_2) \equiv \Big\langle \langle\text{«op»}, \text{«opC»}\rangle,\ \langle\text{«op1»}, o_1\rangle,\ \langle\text{«op2»}, o_2\rangle \Big\rangle$$

19.3.3 – And equivalent specifiers for other commonly used operations:

$$E_\sigma(o_1) \equiv \Big\langle \langle\text{«op»}, \text{«opE»}\rangle,\ \langle\text{«op1»}, o_1\rangle \Big\rangle$$

$$C_{1\sigma}(o_1) \equiv \Big\langle \langle\text{«op»}, \text{«opC»}\rangle,\ \langle\text{«op1»}, o_1\rangle \Big\rangle$$

$$C_{3\sigma}(o_1, o_2, o_3) \equiv \Big\langle \langle\text{«op»}, \text{«opC»}\rangle,\ \langle\text{«op1»}, o_1\rangle,\ \langle\text{«op2»}, o_2\rangle,\ \langle\text{«op3»}, o_3\rangle \Big\rangle$$

$$Y_\sigma(o_1, o_2) \equiv \Big\langle \langle \text{«op»}, \text{«opY»} \rangle, \ \langle \text{«op1»}, o_1 \rangle, \ \langle \text{«op2»}, o_2 \rangle \Big\rangle$$

$$X_\sigma(o_1, o_2) \equiv \Big\langle \langle \text{«op»}, \text{«opX»} \rangle, \ \langle \text{«op1»}, o_1 \rangle, \ \langle \text{«op2»}, o_2 \rangle \Big\rangle$$

$$T_\sigma(o_1, o_2, o_3) \equiv \Big\langle \langle \text{«op»}, \text{«opT»} \rangle, \ \langle \text{«op1»}, o_1 \rangle, \ \langle \text{«op2»}, o_2 \rangle, \ \langle \text{«op3»}, o_3 \rangle \Big\rangle$$

$$H_{0_\sigma}(o_1) \equiv \Big\langle \langle \text{«op»}, \text{«op+H0»} \rangle, \ \langle \text{«op1»}, o_1 \rangle \Big\rangle$$

$$H_{0_\sigma}^{-1}(o_1) \equiv \Big\langle \langle \text{«op»}, \text{«op-H0»} \rangle, \ \langle \text{«op1»}, o_1 \rangle \Big\rangle$$

19.3.4 – Operation specifiers are used to specify new «instruction»'s within «configurations».

19.3.5 – There is one additional operation specifier for recursive evaluation of machines:

$$R_\sigma(o_1) \equiv \Big\langle \langle \text{«op»}, \text{«R»} \rangle, \ \langle \text{«op1»}, o_1 \rangle \Big\rangle$$

19.4 Refs

19.4.1 – In order for these structures to have proper context, we also require a new concept type called a *ref*. A ref refers to a component of the emulated machine's «structure».

19.4.2 – Refs have their own specifier, indicated by ρ:

$$\rho(r) \equiv \langle \text{«ref»}, r \rangle$$

19.4.3 – For example, imagine our «structure» looks like this:

$$\Big\langle \langle \text{«ex»}, \text{«A»} \rangle \Big\rangle$$

19.4.4 – In this case, $R(\rho(\text{«}ex\text{»})) \to \text{«A»}$.

19.4.5 – Refs are crucially important, because they allow us to refer back to the current machine state, and define transformations on it.

19.5 Instruction Specifier

19.5.1 – We will define one more specifier that prepares a specified operation specified to be evaluated recursively, ϵ:

$$\epsilon(s, c, o) \equiv \Big\langle \langle \text{«structure»}, s \rangle, \langle \text{«configurations»}, c \rangle, \ \langle \text{«operation»}, o \rangle \Big\rangle$$

19.5.2 – We will see how this structure will allow us to pass down the current emulated machine state, via «structure» and «configurations», down recursive levels of operation execution so that it can be accessed by refs embedded down the operation hierarchy. This will become more clear as we build out our machine.

19.6 Example Machine

19.6.1 – Now that we have our universal machine structure and necessary specifiers defined, let's give an example of a simple machine, so we can see what our targeted representation will look like. This will give us a clearer idea of how the relations we define between machine states emulates the represented machine.

19.6.2 – Our example, machine $\mathcal{M}_q$, we will straightforwardly compose the component tagged by «ex», with another concept «B»:

19.6.3 – First, our specifier:

$$\sigma_q(a, b, r) \equiv \Big\langle \langle \text{«op1»}, a \rangle, \ \langle \text{«op2»}, b \rangle, \ \langle \text{«result»}, r \rangle \Big\rangle$$

19.6.4 – And now our single relation:

$$s_{0_q} = \sigma_q([\,], [\,], [\cdot])$$

$$R(s_{0_q}) \to \sigma_q([\,], \ [\,], \langle s_{0_q}[\text{op1}], s_{0_q}[\text{op1}] \rangle)$$

19.6.5 – For example:

$$R(\sigma_q(\text{«A»}, \text{«B»}, [\,])) \to \sigma_q([\,], [\,], \langle \text{«A»}, \text{«B»} \rangle)$$

$$R(\sigma_q(\text{«apple»}, \text{«banana»})) \to \sigma_q([\,], [\,], \langle \text{«apple»}, \text{«banana»} \rangle)$$

19.7 Example Universal Machine Structure

19.7.1 – Now let's represent $R(\sigma_q(\text{«A»}, \text{«B»}, [\,]))$ as a universal machine.

19.7.2 – First let's create a new type of specifier, a *relation specifier*, to denote the transformation that should occur from a given machine state in terms of a structure built from *operation specifiers*.

19.7.3 – *Relation specifiers* will be notated with ω, in this case ω_q.

$$\omega_q(a, b, r) \equiv C_{3\sigma}\Big(C_{2\sigma}(\text{«op1»}, a),\ C_{2\sigma}(\text{«op2»}, b),\ C_{2\sigma}(\text{«result»}, r)\Big)$$

19.7.4 – This the direct analog of σ_q from §19.6.3 above.

19.7.5 – We will show in §19.10 that relations have an isomorphic mapping to relations specifiers; that is, that every relation maps in a structure-preserving way to exactly one relation specifier, and vice versa.

19.7.6 – Now let's show the structure of our universal machine:

$$\mathcal{M}_U(s_q, c_q) \to r_q$$

$$: s_q = \sigma_q(\text{«A»}, \text{«B»}, [\,])$$

$$: c_{q_0} = \sigma_q([\,], [\,], [\cdot]) \xrightarrow[c_U]{} \omega_q\Big([\,],\ [\,],\ C_{2\sigma}(\rho(\text{«op1»}), \rho(\text{«op2»}))\Big)$$

$$: r_q = \mathcal{M}_{U_r}\Big(\sigma_q([\,], [\,], \langle\text{«A»}, \text{«B»}\rangle)\Big)$$

19.7.7 – What this formula does is:

1. Sets the machine state in «structure» to $\sigma_q(\text{«A»}, \text{«B»}, [\,])$;
2. Creates a single configuration c_{q_0} in «configurations» at index «0»;
3. That configuration looks for any «structure» that matches $\sigma_q([\,], [\,], [\cdot])$ (i.e. its «pattern»);
4. When a match is found, the outer ω_q is used to reconstruct «structure», and the operation indicated by $C_{2\sigma}(\rho(\text{«op1»}), \rho(\text{«op2»}))$ is executed, yielding $\langle\text{«A»}, \text{«B»}\rangle$ in r_q.

19.7.8 – Note that the structure specified by $C_{2\sigma}$ represents the operation C with two arguments, $C_{3\sigma}$ with three, etc.

19.7.9 – Embedded within that operation are the refs $\rho(\text{«op1»})$ and $\rho(\text{«op2»})$, which in this case refers to the «A» and «B» in «structure», respectively.

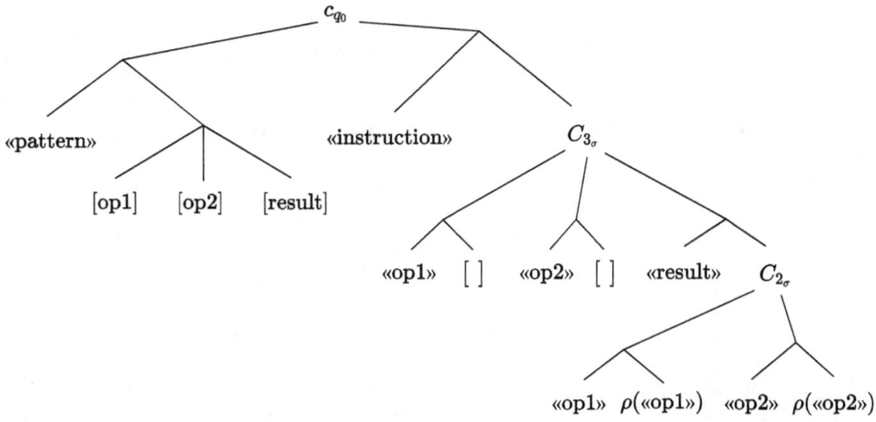

Figure 43: *Example Configuration:* This structure represents a configuration that combines the inputs from two operands, «op1» and «op2», via operation C, indicated by $C_{2\sigma}$, into its «result».

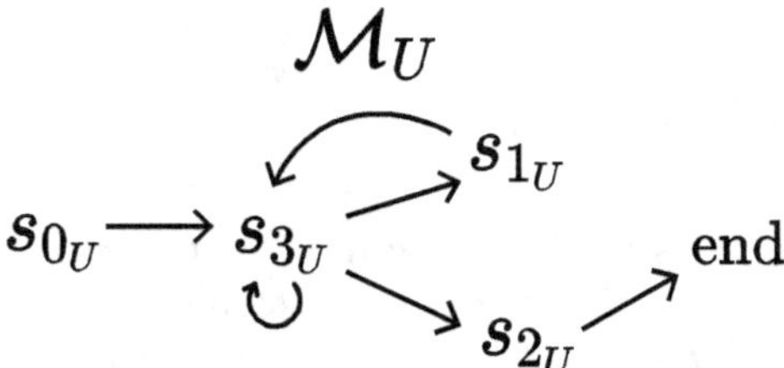

Figure 44: *Evaluation Cycle State Graph:* This graph shows that s_{3_U} repeats until «structure» matches the current «configuration»'s «pattern». When a match is found, s_{1_U} evaluates the «instruction» and resets the state to s_{3_U}, which will again look for another match. When no further matches are found, s_{2_U} is invoked and the cycle completes.

19.8 Evaluation Cycle

19.8.1 – Now that we have a picture of how we want our universal machine to be structured, we can now put into place the relations we need for the core of the machine, which we will call the *evaluation cycle*.

19.8.2 – We need to traverse «configurations» until we find one whose «pattern» matches «structure». When we find a match, we will evaluate the structure that represents the operation to be applied.

19.8.3 – Our first state will initialize the machine:

$$s_{0_U} = \sigma_U([\,], [\,], [\cdot], [\,], [\,], [\cdot], [\cdot])$$

$$R(s_{0_U}) \to \sigma_U\Big(s_{0_U}[\text{structure}],\ s_{0_U}[\text{configurations}],\ «0»,$$
$$s_{0_U}[\text{configurations}][0],\ «\text{false}»,\ [\,],\ [\,]\Big)$$

19.8.4 – Our second state will evaluate the previous «instruction» if the previous configuration is «matched»; evaluation is represented by a new operation V, which will be defined below.

$$s_{1_U} = \sigma_U([\,], [\,], «\text{any-num}», [\,], «\text{true}», [\,], [\cdot])$$

$$R(s_{1_U}) \to \sigma_U\Big(V(s_{1_U}[\text{structure}], s_{1_U}[\text{configurations}], s_{1_U}[\text{instruction}]),$$
$$s_{1_U}[\text{configurations}],\ «0»,\ s_{1_U}[\text{configurations}][0],\ «\text{false}»,\ [\,],\ [\,]\Big)$$

19.8.5 – Note that after the operation has been evaluated, it sets the «index» back to «0», setting the machine up to restart the evaluation cycle.

19.8.6 – Our third state cleans up the machine and moves «structure» to «result» if there is no «next» instruction:

$$s_{2_U} = \sigma_U([\,], [\,], «\text{any-num}», [\cdot], [\,], [\,], [\,])$$

$$R(s_{2_U}) \to \sigma_U([\,], [\,], [\,], [\,], [\,], [\,], s_{2_U}[\text{structure}])$$

19.8.7 – Our final state moves to the next instruction, if the current instruction does not match «structure».

19.8.8 – As it makes this iteration, it must set «matched» and «instruction» to the appropriate values, given the current configuration indicated by «index».

$$s_{3_U} = \sigma_U([\,], [\,], \text{«any-num»}, [\,], \text{«false»}, [\,], [\cdot])$$

$$R(s_{3_U}) \to \sigma_U\Big(s_{3_U}[\text{structure}],\ s_{3_U}[\text{configurations}],$$

$$H_0(s_{3_U}[\text{index}]),\ s_{3_U}[\text{configurations}][H_0(s_{3_U}[\text{index}])],$$

$$Y(s_{3_U}[\text{structure}], s_{3_U}[\text{configurations}][s_{3_U}[\text{index}]][\text{pattern}]),$$

$$s_{3_U}[\text{configurations}][s_{3_U}[\text{index}]][\text{instruction}],\ [\,]\Big)$$

19.9 Evaluation

19.9.1 – With the evaluation loop in place, now we need to define how the operations themselves are evaluated.

19.9.2 – Let's start by defining how each operation indicated in §19.3 should be applied.

19.9.3 – To illustrate, let's look at $C_{1\sigma}$:

$$s_{C_1} = \epsilon([\,],\ [\,],\ C_{1\sigma}([\,]))$$

$$R(s_{C_1}) \to \epsilon\Big(s_{C_1}[\text{structure}],\ s_{C_1}[\text{configurations}],$$

$$C(V(s_{C_1}[\text{structure}],\ s_{C_1}[\text{configurations}],\ s_{C_1}[\text{operation}][\text{op1}]))\Big)$$

19.9.4 – The first two arguments to the instruction specifier ϵ are «structure» and «configurations». This allows us to inject that same machine state into operation V, *evaluate*, which yields recursive evaluation of the specified operations.

19.9.5 – The final argument is the «operation», a structural representation of the operation that will be performed, which will be transformed into the result of the operation.

19.9.6 – Let's now define operation V:

$$V(s, c, o) \equiv X(R(\epsilon(s, c, o)),\ \text{«operation»})$$

19.9.7 – As we can see, V converts its arguments to an *instruction specifier* with ϵ, then evaluates the operation given with R, and yields the resulting «operation», which will now be the actual result of applying that operation recursively.

19.9.8 – This gives us the capability to nest operations and refs indefinitely, as we could in any other relation.

19.9.9 – For completeness, we'll now give the definitions of each of the remaining common operations:

$$s_{C_2} = \epsilon([\,], [\,], C_{2\sigma}([\,],[\,]))$$

$$R(s_{C_2}) \rightarrow \epsilon\Big(s_{C_2}[\text{structure}], \ s_{C_2}[\text{configurations}],$$
$$C\Big(V(s_{C_2}[\text{structure}], \ s_{C_2}[\text{configurations}], \ s_{C_2}[\text{operation}][\text{op1}]),$$
$$V(s_{C_2}[\text{structure}], \ s_{C_2}[\text{configurations}], \ s_{C_2}[\text{operation}][\text{op2}]))\Big)$$

$$s_{C_3} = \epsilon([\,], [\,], C_{3\sigma}([\,],[\,],[\,]))$$

$$R(s_{C_3}) \rightarrow \epsilon\Big(s_{C_3}[\text{structure}], \ s_{C_3}[\text{configurations}],$$
$$C\Big(V(s_{C_3}[\text{structure}], \ s_{C_3}[\text{configurations}], \ s_{C_3}[\text{operation}][\text{op1}]),$$
$$V(s_{C_3}[\text{structure}], \ s_{C_3}[\text{configurations}], \ s_{C_3}[\text{operation}][\text{op2}]),$$
$$V(s_{C_3}[\text{structure}], \ s_{C_3}[\text{configurstions,}] \ s_{C_3}[\text{operation}][\text{op3}]))\Big)$$

$$s_Y = \epsilon([\,], [\,], Y_\sigma([\,],[\,]))$$

$$R(s_Y) \rightarrow \epsilon\Big(s_Y[\text{structure}], \ s_Y[\text{configurations}],$$
$$Y\Big(V(s_Y[\text{structure}], \ s_Y[\text{configurations}], \ s_Y[\text{operation}][\text{op1}]),$$
$$V(s_Y[\text{structure}], \ s_Y[\text{configurations}], \ s_Y[\text{operation}][\text{op2}]))\Big)$$

$$s_X = \epsilon([\,], [\,], X_\sigma([\,],[\,]))$$

$$R(s_X) \rightarrow \epsilon\Big(s_X[\text{structure}], \ s_X[\text{configurations}],$$
$$X\Big(V(s_X[\text{structure}], \ s_X[\text{configurations}], \ s_X[\text{operation}][\text{op1}]),$$
$$V(s_X[\text{structure}], \ s_X[\text{configurations}], \ s_X[\text{operation}][\text{op2}]))\Big)$$

$$s_T = \epsilon([\,], [\,], T_\sigma([\,],[\,],[\,]))$$

$$R(s_T) \rightarrow \epsilon\Big(s_T[\text{structure}], \ s_T[\text{configurations}],$$
$$T\Big(V(s_T[\text{structure}], \ V(s_T[\text{configurations}], \ s_T[\text{operation}][\text{op1}]),$$
$$V(s_T[\text{structure}], \ V(s_T[\text{configurations}], \ s_T[\text{operation}][\text{op2}]),$$
$$V(s_T[\text{structure}], \ V(s_T[\text{configurations}], \ s_T[\text{operation}][\text{op3}]))\Big)$$

$$s_{H_0} = \epsilon([\ ],\ [\ ],\ H_{0_\sigma}([\ ]))$$

$$R(s_{H_0}) \rightarrow \epsilon\Big(s_{H_0}[\text{structure}],\ s_{H_0}[\text{configurations}],$$
$$H_0(V(s_{H_0}[\text{structure}],\ s_{H_0}[\text{configurations}],\ s_{H_0}[\text{operation}][\text{op1}]))\Big)$$

$$s_{H_0^{-1}} = \epsilon([\ ],\ [\ ],\ H_{0_\sigma}^{-1}([\ ]))$$

$$R(s_{H_0^{-1}}) \rightarrow \epsilon\Big(s_{H_0^{-1}}[\text{structure}],\ s_{H_0^{-1}}[\text{configurations}],$$
$$H_0^{-1}(V(s_{H_0^{-1}}[\text{structure}],\ s_{H_0^{-1}}[\text{configurations}],\ s_{H_0^{-1}}[\text{operation}][\text{op1}]))\Big)$$

19.9.10 – In addition to our operations, we also need to define how to evaluate refs:

$$s_{\text{ref}} = \epsilon([\ ],\ [\ ],\ \rho([\ ]))$$

$$R(s_{\text{ref}}) \rightarrow \epsilon\Big(s_{\text{ref}}[\text{structure}],\ s_{\text{ref}}[\text{configurations}],$$
$$X(s_{\text{ref}}[\text{structure}], s_{\text{ref}}[\text{ref}])\Big)$$

19.9.11 – And finally, a way to recursively evaluate sub-machines:

$$s_R = \epsilon([\ ],\ [\ ],\ R_\sigma([\ ]))$$

$$R(s_R) \rightarrow \epsilon\Big(s_R[\text{structure}],\ s_R[\text{configurations}],$$
$$X\Big(R(V(s_R[\text{structure}],\ s_R[\text{configurations}], s_R[\text{instruction}][\text{instruction}]),$$
$$\text{«result»})\Big)\Big)$$

19.9.12 – This recursive evaluation procedure allows us to simulate any conceptual machine, or compound conceptual machine, in a format that is isomorphic to evaluated conceptual machine.

19.10 Isomorphism

19.10.1 – When we say that the universal machine is isomorphic to the base-level machines, what we mean is that there exists an exact one-to-one mapping that can convert one to the other and vice-versa. This mapping must also preserve the structure of the representation between the two types of machines.

19.10.2 – In our case, this mapping consists of a set of substitution rules, which can be implemented in a mechanical way.

19.10.3 – Because of the form that we designed our universal machine to take, we can define these substitutions rather simply.

19.10.4 – We must keep in mind that these results assume that the relations are defined in a normalized form: all extractions will be denoted with operation X instead of the alternate bracketed syntax, and all specifiers and complex operations will be expanded to substitute their implementation as the fundamental operations (except for H_0 and H_0^{-1} which we have also defined operation specifiers for).

19.10.5 – The procedure works for the conversion between some base machine $\mathcal{M}_b$ to a state that can be evaluated by our universal machine $\mathcal{M}_U$ like this:

1. Begin by setting «structure» in $\mathcal{M}_U$ to some valid initial state of $\mathcal{M}_b$;
2. For every relation r, of every state s in M_b:
    1. Create a new configuration c_r of «configurations» in $\mathcal{M}_U$;
    2. Set $c_r[\text{pattern}] = s$;
    3. Set $c_r[\text{instruction}]$ equal to the result of $R(s)$, transformed according to the substitution rules below.

19.10.6 – The table below represents the substitution rules to transform the result of a relation into a concept that represents the operation.

$R(s)$	$c_r[\text{instruction}]$
$X(s,[\,]_1)$	$\rho([\,]_1)$
$E([\,]_1)$	$E_\sigma([\,]_1)$
$C([\,]_1)$	$C_{1\sigma}([\,]_1)$
$C([\,]_1, [\,]_2)$	$C_{2\sigma}([\,]_1, [\,]_2)$
$C([\,]_1, [\,]_2, [\,]_3)$	$C_{3\sigma}([\,]_1, [\,]_2, [\,]_3)$
$Y([\,]_1, [\,]_2)$	$Y_\sigma([\,]_1, [\,]_2)$
$X([\,]_1, [\,]_2)$	$X_\sigma([\,]_1, [\,]_2)$
$T([\,]_1, [\,]_2, [\,]_3)$	$T_\sigma([\,]_1, [\,]_2, [\,]_3)$
$H_0([\,]_1)$	$H_{0_\sigma}([\,]_1)$
$H_0^{-1}([\,]_1)$	$H_{0_\sigma}^{-1}([\,]_1)$
$R([\,]_1)$	$R_\sigma([\,]_1)$

19.10.7 – The substitution rules use the proxy [ ] as a placeholder for a conceptual entity, marked with a subscript to identify the particular entity between both sides of the transformation.

19.10.8 – This is the entire set of every fundamental operation in our system.

19.10.9 – In the opposite direction, the procedure goes:

1. Begin by setting initial state of $\mathcal{M}_b$ to «structure» in $\mathcal{M}_U$;
2. For every configuration c_r, of «configurations» in $\mathcal{M}_U$:
    1. Create a new state $s = c_r[\text{pattern}]$;
    2. Define a relation $R(s)$, transformed from $c_r[\text{instruction}]$ according to the substitution rules below.

19.10.10 – This table is the exact inverse of the one in §19.10.6:

$c_r[\text{instruction}]$	$R(s)$
$\rho([\,]_1)$	$X(s,[\,]_1)$
$E_\sigma([\,]_1)$	$E([\,]_1)$
$C_{1\sigma}([\,]_1)$	$C([\,]_1)$
$C_{2\sigma}([\,]_1,[\,]_2)$	$C([\,]_1,[\,]_2)$
$C_{3\sigma}([\,]_1,[\,]_2,[\,]_3)$	$C([\,]_1,[\,]_2,[\,]_3)$
$Y_\sigma([\,]_1,[\,]_2)$	$Y([\,]_1,[\,]_2)$
$X_\sigma([\,]_1,[\,]_2)$	$X([\,]_1,[\,]_2)$
$T_\sigma([\,]_1,[\,]_2,[\,]_3)$	$T([\,]_1,[\,]_2,[\,]_3)$
$H_{0_\sigma}([\,]_1)$	$H_0([\,]_1)$
$H_{0_\sigma}^{-1}([\,]_1)$	$H_0^{-1}([\,]_1)$
$R_\sigma([\,]_1)$	$R([\,]_1)$

19.10.11 – Our substitution rules map every operation from base-level machines to universal machines, and vice versa; each configuration from the universal machine is mapped isomorphically to a relation in a base machine, and vice versa.

19.10.12 – These two conditions guarantee that our universal machine is truly universal—i.e. that every base-level conceptual machine has an equivalent universal machine state.

19.11 Multiplication Machine

19.11.1 – Let's build another more complicated machine to show the full capabilities of our universal machine by demonstrating the analogue of the multiplying machine M_{2_c} within our universal machine.

19.11.2 – Let's first take a look at the state specifier σ_{2_c} from §13.3.2:

$$\sigma_{2_c}(o_1, o_2, r) = \Big\langle \langle \text{«op1»}, o_1 \rangle, \ \langle \text{«op2»}, o_2 \rangle, \ \langle \text{«product»}, r \rangle \Big\rangle$$

19.11.3 – Now we'll define our relation specifier ω_{2_c} to match:

$$\omega_{2_c}(o_1, o_2, r) \equiv C_{3\sigma}\Big(C_{2\sigma}(\text{«op1»}, a), \ C_{2\sigma}(\text{«op2»}, b), \ C_{2\sigma}(\text{«product»}, r) \Big)$$

19.11.4 – Our machine will give a representation of the multiplication 2×3. Here's our operation:

$$\mathcal{M}_U(s_{2c}, c_{2c}) \to r_{2c}$$

$$: s_{2c} = \sigma_{2_c}(\text{«2»}, \text{«3»}, [\,])$$

19.11.5 – We'll look at our machine states one-by-one, and compare them with the analogous states from M_{2_c}. Let's look at the first state $s_{0_{2c}}$, from §13.3.3:

$$s_{0_{2c}} = \sigma_{2_c}\Big([\,],[\,],[\cdot]\Big)$$

$$R(s_{0_{2c}}) \to \sigma_{2_c}\Big(s_{0_{2c}}[\text{op1}], \ s_{0_{2c}}[\text{op2}], \ \text{«0»}\Big)$$

19.11.6 – Here's our analogue in the universal machine for comparison:

$$: c_{2c_0} = \sigma_{2_c}([\,], \ [\,], \ [\cdot]) \xrightarrow[c_U]{} \omega_{2_c}\Big(\rho(\text{«op1»}), \ \rho(\text{«op2»}), \ \text{«0»}\Big)$$

19.11.7 – Now let's look at the second state, $s_{1_{2c}}$, from §13.3.4:

$$s_{1_{2c}} = \sigma_{2_c}\Big([\,], \text{«not-0»}, [\,]\Big)$$

$$R(s_{1_{2c}}) \to \sigma_{2_c}\Big(s_{1_{2c}}[\text{op1}], \ H_0^{-1}(s_{1_{2c}}[\text{op2}]), \ H_{1_c}(s_{1_{2c}}[\text{product}], s_{1_{2c}}[\text{op1}])\Big)$$

19.11.8 – Interestingly, this one invokes H_{1_c}, an operation defined by the addition machine from §13.2. The way we handle that is to then translate the addition machine states right into our universal machine.

19.11.9 – Now, we need our addition state specifier σ_{1_c}, defined in §13.2.2:

$$\sigma_{1_c}(o_1, o_2, r) = \Big\langle \langle \text{«op1»}, o_1 \rangle,\ \langle \text{«op2»}, o_2 \rangle,\ \langle \text{«sum»}, r \rangle \Big\rangle$$

19.11.10 – Let's create the equivalent relation specifier:

$$\omega_{1_c}(o_1, o_2, r) \equiv C_{3\sigma}\Big(C_{2\sigma}(\text{«op1»}, a),\ C_{2\sigma}(\text{«op2»}, b),\ C_{2\sigma}(\text{«sum»}, r)\Big)$$

19.11.11 – Now, let's translate the first addition machine state $s_{0_{c1}}$ from §13.2.3:

$$s_{0_{c1}} = \sigma_{1_c}\Big([\,], \ [\,], \ [\cdot]\Big)$$

$$R(s_{0_{c1}}) \to \sigma_{1_c}\Big([\,], \ s_{0_{c1}}[\text{op2}], \ s_{0_{c1}}[\text{op1}]\Big)$$

19.11.12 – We define its equivalent in $\mathcal{M}_U$:

$$: c_{2c_1} = \sigma_{1_c}([\,], \ [\,], \ [\cdot]) \underset{c_U}{\to} \omega_{1_c}\Big([\,], \rho(\text{«op2»}), \ \rho(\text{«op1»})\Big)$$

19.11.13 – Now $s_{1_{c1}}$ from §13.2.4:

$$s_{1_{c1}} = \sigma_{1_c}\Big([\cdot], \ \text{«not-0»}, \ [\,]\Big)$$

$$R(s_{1_{c1}}) \to \sigma_{1_c}\Big([\,], \ H_0^{-1}(s_{1_{c1}}[\text{op2}]), \ H_0(s_{1_{c1}}[\text{sum}])\Big)$$

19.11.14 – Its equivalent:

$$: c_{2c_2} = \sigma_{1_c}([\cdot], \ \text{«not-0»}, \ [\,]) \underset{c_U}{\to} \omega_{1_c}\Big([\,], \ H_{0_\sigma}^{-1}(\rho(\text{«op2»})), \ H_{0_\sigma}(\rho(\text{«sum»}))\Big)$$

19.11.15 – And $s_{2_{c1}}$ from §13.2.6:

$$s_{2_{c1}} = \sigma_{1_c}\Big([\cdot], \ \text{«}\dot{0}\text{»}, \ [\,]\Big)$$

$$R(s_{2_{c1}}) \rightarrow \sigma_{1_c}\Big([\,], \,[\,], \, s_{2_{c1}}[\text{sum}]\Big)$$

19.11.16 – Translated:

$$: c_{2c_3} = \sigma_{1_c}([\cdot], \, \text{«not-0»}, \, [\,]) \underset{c_U}{\rightarrow} \omega_{1_c}\Big([\,], \,[\,], \, \rho(\text{«sum»})\Big)$$

19.11.17 – We now have all the states we need within M_U to handle the operation H_{1_c} from §19.11.7. Let's first look at the definition of H_{1_c} from §13.2.8:

$$H_{1_c}(o_1, o_2) \equiv X\Big(R(\mathcal{M}_{1_c}(o_1, o_2)), \, \text{«sum»}\Big)$$

19.11.18 – Since $\mathcal{M}_{1_c}(o_1, o_2) \equiv \sigma_{1_c}(o_1, o_2, [\,])$, according to §13.2.7, this can be translated according to our substitution rules to:

$$H_{1_\sigma}(o_1, o_2) \equiv X_\sigma\Big(R_\sigma(\omega_{1_c}(o_1, o_2, [\,])), \, \text{«sum»}\Big)$$

19.11.19 – Now we can define the $\mathcal{M}_U$ equivalent of §19.11.7:

$$: c_{2c_4} = \sigma_{2_c}\Big([\,], \, \text{«not-0»}, [\,]\Big) \underset{c_U}{\rightarrow} \omega_{2_c}\Big(\rho(\text{«op1»}), \, H_{0_\sigma}^{-1}(\rho(\text{«op2»})),$$
$$H_{1_\sigma}(\rho(\text{«product»}), \rho(\text{«op1»}))\Big)$$

19.11.20 – Let's translate the final state $s_{2_{c2}}$ from §13.3.6:

$$s_{2_{c2}} = \sigma_{2_c}\Big([\,], \, \text{«}\dot{0}\text{»}, [\,]\Big)$$

$$R(s_{2_{c2}}) \rightarrow \sigma_{2_c}\Big([\,], \,[\,], \, s_{2_{c2}}[\text{product}]\Big)$$

19.11.21 – Our final configuration:

$$: c_{2c_5} = \sigma_{2_c}\Big([\,], \, \text{«}\dot{0}\text{»}, [\,]\Big) \underset{c_U}{\rightarrow} \omega_{2_c}\Big([\,], \,[\,], \, \rho(\text{«product»})\Big)$$

19.11.22 – And our expected result of 2×3:

$$: r_{2c} = M_{U_r}(\sigma_{2_c}([\,], [\,], \text{«6»}))$$

19.12 Operation U

19.12.1 – It will be useful to have an operation that represents the evaluation of arbitrary states and configurations of $\mathcal{M}_U$.

19.12.2 – We'll define operation U to execute arbitrary $\mathcal{M}$ machine states and configuration sets as:

$$U(s, c) \equiv X(R(\mathcal{M}_U(s, c)), \text{«result»})$$

20 Abstraction

"So intelligence, which is to say, generalization power, is literally sensitivity to abstract analogies, and that's in fact all there is to it."

— François Chollet

The defining character of the human mind is its ability to extract clarity from confusion—an abstract reality from a wholly concrete one.

20.1 Redundancy & Comparison

20.1.1 – Recall our definition of abstraction from §1.4.1:

> An *abstraction* is a construction which models multiple things, or aspects of things, as a single thing.

20.1.2 – This mapping of many things to a single thing is a compressive operation, from an information perspective. We are representing the same information with a smaller set of elements.

20.1.3 – Similar to compression in information theory, the compression occurs by identifying redundancy between two representations, and creates a new, more terse representation that can apply to both.

20.1.4 – In order to perform this type of operation, we need a way of determining how similar two concepts are, and to extract those similarities.

20.1.5 – For this purpose, we will define an alternate version of Υ—Υ^*—which returns a numerical representation of how similar conceptual structures are.

20.1.6 – This section will demonstrate how we could give a plausible definition of Υ^*, but it is in no way definitive that this is the definition that is most accurate or useful. Particularly it has a naive implementation with very poor scaling properties, but it has other properties that may make other approaches more desirable as well. This is left to future work to sort out.

20.1.7 – In order to do create a numerical value for the comparison, we first need to come up with some alternate representation of a conceptual structure that is more amenable to comparison. We'll accomplish this by splitting a conceptual structure into a set of every possible substructure:

$$g(a) \equiv g'(a) \cup g''(g'(a))$$

$$g'(a) \equiv \bigcup_{b \in E(a)} \begin{cases} \mathcal{P}(\{b\}) & \text{if } \Pi(b) \\ \{C(c) : c \in \{g'(b_1) \times \ldots \times g'(b_n)\},\ b_i \in E(b)\} & \text{otherwise} \end{cases}$$

$$g''(A) \equiv \bigcup_{a \in A} \begin{cases} \{\} & \text{if } \Pi(a) \\ E(a) \cup g''(E(a)) & \text{if } |E(a)| = 1 \\ \{\} & \text{otherwise} \end{cases}$$

20.1.8 – $g(a)$ gives every possible substructure of a. It does this via the union of the results of the two subfunctions g' and g''.

20.1.9 – $g'(a)$ gives a set of every possible substructure of the same depth as a. g' iterates over every component b of a. If the component b is primitive, i.e. $\Pi(b)$, then it returns the powerset of $\{b\}$, i.e. $\{b, \{\}\}$. Otherwise, every combination of g' acting on each component of b is returned, recursively processing all non-primary concepts in the tree.

20.1.10 – Let's look at an example with a simple concept x, where:

$$x = \langle q, r \rangle$$

$$g'(x) = \{\langle q, r \rangle, \langle q \rangle, \langle r \rangle\}$$

20.1.11 – Notice that this gives us every possible substructure of the same depth. But it *does not* yield to us the substructures at lower levels, q and r in this case.

20.1.12 – For that reason we have $g''(A)$ which takes the set of structures yielded by g' and traverses down them each time the structure has only one, non-primitive child.

20.1.13 – Let's look at $g''(g'(x))$ the example from above:

$$g''(\{\langle q, r \rangle, \langle q \rangle, \langle r \rangle\}) = \{q, r\}$$

20.1.14 – And we can now see that $g(x)$ returns every substructure of x:

$$g(x) = \{\langle q, r \rangle, \langle q \rangle, \langle r \rangle, q, r\}$$

20.1.15 – If you are following closely, you may notice that this some hidden logic here that is used to remove empty concepts and sets of concepts, which I have omitted for clarity.

20.1.16 – For our example, we will also utilize a similar conceptual structure y, which only differs from x in that x's r becomes an s.

$$y = \langle q, s \rangle$$

$$g(y) = \{\langle q, s \rangle, \langle q \rangle, \langle s \rangle, q, s\}$$

20.1.17 – Now we define $g_\cup(A)$, function that will gather a set of every permutation in the set of concepts A.

$$g_\cup(A) \equiv \bigcup_{a \in A} g(a)$$

20.1.18 – In our example:

$$g_\cup(\{x,y\}) = \{\langle q,r\rangle, \langle q,s\rangle, \langle q\rangle, \langle r\rangle, \langle s\rangle, q, r, s\}$$

20.1.19 – We will refer to each potential substructure as a *permutation*.

20.1.20 – The function $d(p,a)$ below takes a permutation p and a concept a; it returns 1 in the case that p exists in a's set of permutations $g(a)$ and 0 otherwise:

$$d(p,a) \equiv \begin{cases} 1 & \text{if } p \in g(a) \\ 0 & \text{otherwise} \end{cases}$$

20.1.21 – The functions $g(a)$, $g_\cup(A)$, and $d(p,a)$ allow us to construct a set $e(a \mid A)$ for concept a of set A, indexed by each permutation p from $g_\cup(A)$ which has the value 1 when $p \in g(a)$ and 0 otherwise. This representation as a binary string is amenable to further quantitative analysis.

20.1.22 – First we can look at the binary representation of a concept without respect to any other set of concepts.

20.1.23 – In this case, every value in the binary string will be 1 because the set is indexed by those permutations that *are* in $g(a)$. For a concept a we denote this:

$$e(a) \equiv \{1_p\}_{p \in g(a)}$$

20.1.24 – In an alternative formulation, we can look at this representation with respect to the permutations generated from a set of concepts A as $e(a \mid A)$:

$$e(a \mid A) \equiv \{\, d(p,a)_p \,\}_{p \in g_\cup(A)}$$

20.1.25 – Following our example of x and y, let's look at $e(x)$, $e(y)$, $e(x \mid \{x,y\})$, and $e(y \mid \{x,y\})$:

$$e(x) = \{1_{\langle q,r\rangle}, \ 1_{\langle q\rangle}, \ 1_{\langle r\rangle}, \ 1_q, \ 1_r\}$$

$$e(x \mid \{x,y\}) = \{1_{\langle q,r\rangle}, \ 0_{\langle q,s\rangle}, \ 1_{\langle q\rangle}, \ 1_{\langle r\rangle}, \ 0_{\langle s\rangle}, \ 1_q, \ 1_r, \ 0_s\}$$

$$e(y) = \{1_{\langle q,s\rangle}, \ 1_{\langle q\rangle}, \ 1_{\langle s\rangle}, \ 1_q, \ 1_s\}$$

$$e(y \mid \{x,y\}) = \{0_{\langle q,r\rangle}, \ 1_{\langle q,s\rangle}, \ 1_{\langle q\rangle}, \ 0_{\langle r\rangle}, \ 1_{\langle s\rangle}, \ 1_q, \ 0_r, \ 1_s\}$$

20.1.26 – Our final utility function for defining Υ^* is $m(p, A)$, a function which takes a permutation p and a set of concepts A and returns the mean value of $d(p, a)$ for all values of $a \in A$:

$$m(p, A) \equiv \frac{1}{|A|} \sum_{a \in A} d(p, a)$$

20.1.27 – Note that when all values of $d(p, a)$ for $a \in A$ are 1, $m(p, A) = 1$; when all values are not 1, $0 < m(p, A) < 1$. This is an important property, because we define Υ^* in terms of the Shannon entropy[33] needed to represent the difference between conceptual structures.

20.1.28 – We'll now give our first definition of Υ^* which accepts a set of concepts A and returns the Shannon entropy of the set according to the permutation-indexed binary strings generated by e above.

$$\Upsilon^*(A) \equiv - \sum_{p \in g_\cup(A)} m \, \log_2 m \, + \, (1 - m) \, \log_2 (1 - m)$$

$$: m = m(p, A)$$

20.1.29 – Notice that when all structures in A contain a given permutation p, $m(p, A) = 1$; because $\log_2 1 = 0$, the entropy added for that item is 0. Further, that means that a set of identical structures gives a value of Υ^* that is also 0.

20.1.30 – Let's calculate $\Upsilon^*(\{x, y\})$ from our example above:

$$\Upsilon^*(\{x, y\}) = -3\left(\tfrac{1+0}{2} \, \log_2 \tfrac{1+0}{2} + (1 - \tfrac{1+0}{2}) \, \log_2(1 - \tfrac{1+0}{2}) \right)$$
$$- 3\left(\tfrac{1+0}{2} \, \log_2 \tfrac{1+0}{2} + (1 - \tfrac{1+0}{2}) \, \log_2(1 - \tfrac{1+0}{2}) \right)$$
$$- 2\left(\tfrac{1+1}{2} \, \log_2 \tfrac{1+1}{2} + (1 - \tfrac{1+1}{2}) \, \log_2(1 - \tfrac{1+1}{2}) \right)$$

$$\Upsilon^*(\{x, y\}) = -3\left(.5 \cdot \log_2 .5 + .5 \cdot \log_2 .5 \right)$$
$$- 3\left(.5 \cdot \log_2 .5 + .5 \cdot \log_2 .5 \right)$$
$$- 2\left(1 \cdot \log_2 1 + 0 \cdot \log_2 0 \right)$$

$$\Upsilon^*(\{x, y\}) = (3 \cdot 1) + (3 \cdot 1) + (2 \cdot 0)$$
$$\Upsilon^*(\{x, y\}) = 6$$

---

[33]See Shannon (1948).

20.1.31 – Notice that 6 is the number of bits that are different between $e(x \mid \{x, y\})$ and $e(y \mid \{x, y\})$. Υ^* is a measure of the difference in information between two conceptual structures.

20.1.32 – Because $\{x, y\}$ is a set of only 2 items, the numbers always come out to be whole numbers, but fractional numbers of this measured entropy are also possible.

20.1.33 – We also have two alternate definitions of Υ^*.

20.1.34 – The first accepts two arguments for separate concepts a and b and returns the amount of information required (i.e. how many permutations [bits] need to change) to transform a into a form that will match the structure of b:

$$\Upsilon^*(a \mid b) \equiv - \sum_{p \in g(b)} \log_2 m(p, \{a, b\})$$

20.1.35 – Notice that in this case the sum is over $p \in g(b)$, as opposed to $p \in g_\cup(A)$ from §20.1.28. This also applies to the second alternative definition that immediately follows.

20.1.36 – For example $\Upsilon^*(y \mid x) = 3$, because only the 5 permutations from $g(x)$ are considered, and the permutations $\langle q \rangle$ and q match.

20.1.37 – The second alternative definition of Υ^* is a generalization of the first; it accepts a set of concepts A and another concept b.

20.1.38 – It returns the amount of information required to transform that set of concepts into a form that matches b.

$$\Upsilon^*(A \mid b) \equiv \sum_{a \in A} \Upsilon^*(a \mid b)$$

20.2 Operation W & Productivity

20.2.1 – We'd like a way to find an optimal abstraction of set of conceptual structures. Let's define the optimal abstraction of a set of concepts A as a new operation W, *withdraw*.

$$W(\{a, ...\}) \to b$$

$$W(A) \equiv \arg\max_{p \in g_\cup(A)} Q(p \mid A)$$

20.2.2 – Here $Q(p \mid A)$ indicates the productivity of the concept p with respect to the set of concepts A (see §3.2.2).

20.2.3 – W finds the permutation that yields the greatest productivity.

20.2.4 – The naive version outlined in this chapter represents is a brute force approach that will attempt to use every possible permutation $p \in g_\cup(A)$ and will return the argument p that yields the maximum value of $Q(p \mid A)$.

20.2.5 – In practice, we can be certain that the mind does not use a brute force method of computing its abstractions, but instead uses some heuristics to narrow the search.

20.2.6 – This turns abstraction of an optimization problem to find the most efficient approximation of $\underset{p \in g_\cup(A)}{\arg\max} \, Q(p \mid A)$.

20.2.7 – In order to actually put this concept into use, we need a partly-quantified approximation of Q that can be used to perform calculations.

20.2.8 – We can give a functional approximation of $Q(p \mid A)$ by first prioritizing permutations that exist within all members of A, then by taking the entropy of the set A with respect to its abstraction a with $\Upsilon^*_{\text{avg}}(A \mid a)$, the average entropy per permutation in the abstraction, and scaling it by the ratio of the size of the permutation-wise representation of the abstraction $|g(a)|$ to the permutation-wise representation of the set $|g_\cup(A)|$ represented as k_s.

$$\Upsilon^*_{\text{avg}}(A \mid a) = \frac{\Upsilon^*(A \mid a)}{|g(a)| \cdot |A|}$$

$$k_s = \frac{|g(a)|}{|g_\cup(A)|}$$

$$m_{\text{all}}(p, A) = \begin{cases} 1 & \text{if } m(p, A) = 1 \\ 0 & \text{otherwise} \end{cases}$$

$$\tilde{Q}(p \mid A) \equiv \frac{m_{\text{all}}(p, A)}{h_1} + \frac{k_s \left(1 - \Upsilon^*_{\text{avg}}(A \mid p)\right)}{h_0} \; : \; \tilde{Q}(p \mid A) \approx Q(p \mid A)$$

20.2.9 – Notice that m_{all} returns 1 when abstraction a is a permutation of every concept in A and 0 otherwise. Because this is placed over h_1, this criteria holds ultimate precedence over any value of $\frac{k_s(1 - \Upsilon^*_{\text{avg}}(A|p))}{h_0}$.

20.2.10 – From our example above, we can find the abstraction of $\{x, y\}$ is $\langle q \rangle$ as we might expect:

$$W(\{\langle q, r \rangle, \, \langle q, s \rangle\}) \rightarrow \langle q \rangle$$

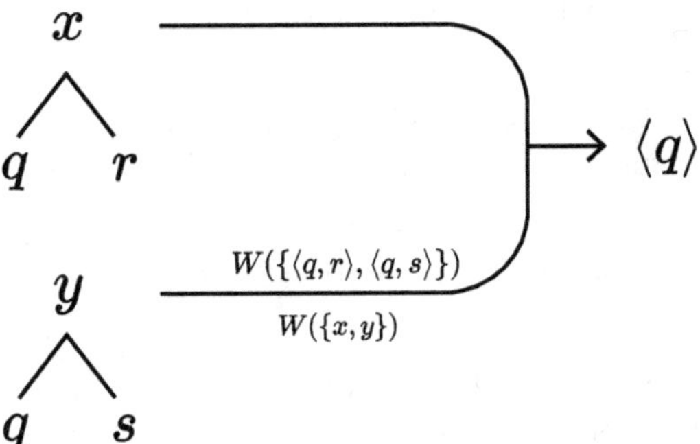

Figure 45: *Abstraction:* Operation W withdraws the abstraction $\langle q \rangle$ as the common substructure of x and y where the value of $Q(\langle q \rangle \mid \{x, y\})$ is the maximum.

20.2.11 – Short of showing the totality of the calculations that lead to this result, the salient ones in this case are:

$$m_{\text{all}}(\langle q \rangle, \{x, y\}) = 1$$

$$k_s \left(1 - \Upsilon^*_{\text{avg}}(\{x, y\} \mid \langle q \rangle)\right) = .25$$

20.3 Analogy

20.3.1 – Another important type of abstraction is analogy. Instead of comparing things directly, the comparison is made between the relation of one set of things and another set of things.

$$A \text{ is to } B \text{ as } C \text{ is to } D.$$

20.3.2 – In our framework we can represent this more directly. An analogy between two sets of concepts holds when a conceptual machine that transforms the first item of the first set to the second item of the first set is the same machine that transforms the first item of the second set to the second item of the second set.

20.3.3 – For example, if we were to say that concept a is to b as c is to d, what we are saying is that there is a machine $\mathcal{M}_x$ such that $\mathcal{M}_x$ acting on a will produce b, and the same $\mathcal{M}_x$ acting on c will produce d:

$$\exists \mathcal{M}_x \left(R(\mathcal{M}_x(a)) \to b \right) \wedge \left(R(\mathcal{M}_x(c)) \to d \right)$$

21 Generalized Machines

"[I]n seeking better ways to learn, this can lead to silent growth in which some better ways to learn may lead to better ways to learn to learn."

— Marvin Minsky

The mechanical structures used in the book can be abstracted, so that techniques that were used in past machines can be put to use toward building generalized machines: machines that build other machines.

21.1 Machine Generalization

21.1.1 – So far we've covered abstraction of conceptual structures via comparison and reduction in redundancy, and abstraction in relationships between structures in terms of analogy.

21.1.2 – The last type of abstraction we will examine is the abstraction of a machine itself: a machine that creates other machines.

21.1.3 – In order to create these abstractions, we will put configurations of universal conceptual machine $\mathcal{M}_U$ to use by representing machines structurally. Then we can apply structural techniques to creating generalizations of those machines.

21.1.4 – We will illustrate this process first by defining a conceptual machine for the arithmetical operation *tetration*, H_4, which is the operation of repeated exponentiation.

21.1.5 – With those configurations in place, we can compare them with those of previous operations for common structure, and create another conceptual machine that can be parameterized to produce sets of configurations for $\mathcal{M}_U$—not only tetration, exponentiation, multiplication, and addition—but for arbitrary hyperoperations, including pentation (H_5, i.e. repeated tetration), etc.

21.2 Tetration Machine

21.2.1 – As is our habit, we begin with our tetration machine specifier σ_{4_c}:

$$\sigma_{4_c}(o_1, o_2, r) \equiv \Big\langle \langle \text{«op1»}, o_1 \rangle, \langle \text{«op2»}, o_2 \rangle, \langle \text{«result4»}, r \rangle \Big\rangle$$

$$: \text{«result4»} = \langle \text{«result»}, \text{«4»} \rangle$$

21.2.2 – Notice that «result4» is equal to the composition of «result» and «4». This is so that we can later create new result concepts for later hyperoperations.

21.2.3 – And now we can begin defining our states. These will largely follow the pattern from §13.4.

21.2.4 – First, we set «result4» to «1»:

$$s_{0_{c4}} = \sigma_{4_c}\Big([\,], \text{«not-0»}, [\cdot]\Big)$$

$$R(s_{0_{c4}}) \to \sigma_{4_c}\Big(s_{0_{c4}}[\text{op1}], \ s_{0_{c4}}[\text{op2}], \text{«1»}\Big)$$

21.2.5 – Our second state takes «result4» to the power «op1» and decrements «op2», so long as «op2» is greater than «0»:

$$s_{1_{c4}} = \sigma_{4_c}\Big([\,], \text{«not-0»}, [\,]\Big)$$

$$R(s_{1_{c4}}) \rightarrow \sigma_{4_c}\Big(s_{1_{c4}}[\text{op1}],\ H_0^{-1}(s_{1_{c4}}[\text{op2}]),\ H_{3_c}(s_{1_{c4}}[\text{result4}], s_{1_{c4}}[\text{op1}])\Big)$$

21.2.6 – And finally we reset «op1» and «op2» to [ ], leaving only «result4», when «op2» is equal to «0».

$$s_{2_{c4}} = \sigma_{4_c}\Big([\,], \text{«}\dot{0}\text{»}, [\,]\Big)$$

$$R(s_{2_{c4}}) \rightarrow \sigma_{4_c}([\,],\ [\,],\ s_{2_{c4}}[\text{result4}])$$

21.2.7 – Below we have our machine specifier and operation:

$$\mathcal{M}_{4_c}(o_1, o_2) \equiv \sigma_{4_c}\Big(o_1, o_2, [\,]\Big)$$

$$H_{4_c}(o_1, o_2) \equiv X\Big(R(\mathcal{M}_{4_c}(o_1, o_2)), \text{«result4»}\Big)$$

21.2.8 – Here's the execution table of $\mathcal{M}_{4_c}(\text{«2»}, \text{«3»})$:

	«op1»	«op2»	«result4»
$\mathcal{M}_{4_c}(\text{«2»}, \text{«3»})$	«2»	«3»	[ ]
$R(s_{0_{c4}}) \rightarrow s_{1_{c4}}$	«2»	«3»	«1»
$R(s_{1_{c4}}) \rightarrow s_{1_{c4}}$	«3»	«3»	«3»
$R(s_{1_{c4}}) \rightarrow s_{1_{c4}}$	«3»	«2»	«9»
$R(s_{1_{c4}}) \rightarrow s_{1_{c4}}$	«3»	«1»	«27»
$R(s_{1_{c4}}) \rightarrow s_{1_{c4}}$	«3»	«0»	«81»
$R(s_{1_{c4}})$	[ ]	[ ]	«81»

21.3 Generalizing Configurations

21.3.1 – We can now put our operation W to use in finding the commonalities between configuration structures, and using them to generalize machines with a wider range of applications and greater productivity.

21.3.2 – We will skip defining a total set of $\mathcal{M}_U$ configurations for $\mathcal{M}_{3_c}$ and $\mathcal{M}_{4_c}$. To illustrate the generalization power provided by operation $\overset{\circ}{W}$ we will compare one configuration from each, the equivalents of $s_{0_{c3}}$ and $s_{0_{c4}}$.

21.3.3 – First, let's look at a configuration structure to represent $s_{0_{c3}}$ (defined in §13.4.3). Notice the use of σ_{c_U} from §19.2.6

$$u_{0_{c3}} = \sigma_{c_U}(p, o)$$

$$: p = \Big\langle \langle «\text{op1}», [\,] \rangle,\ \langle «\text{op2}», [\,] \rangle,\ \langle \langle «\text{result}», «3» \rangle, [\cdot] \rangle \Big\rangle$$

$$: o = C_{3_\sigma}\Big(C_{2_\sigma}(«\text{op1}», \rho(«\text{op2}»)),\ C_{2_\sigma}(«\text{op2}», \rho(«\text{op2}»)),$$

$$C_{2_\sigma}(C_{2_\sigma}(«\text{result}», «3»), «1») \Big)$$

21.3.4 – Let's compare with the extremely similar structure for $s_{0_{c4}}$ from §21.2.4:

$$u_{0_{c4}} = \sigma_{c_U}(p, o)$$

$$: p = \Big\langle \langle «\text{op1}», [\,] \rangle,\ \langle «\text{op2}», [\,] \rangle,\ \langle \langle «\text{result}», «4» \rangle, [\cdot] \rangle \Big\rangle$$

$$: o = C_{3_\sigma}\Big(C_{2_\sigma}(«\text{op1}», \rho(«\text{op2}»)),\ C_{2_\sigma}(«\text{op2}», \rho(«\text{op2}»)),$$

$$C_{2_\sigma}(C_{2_\sigma}(«\text{result}», «4»), «1») \Big)$$

21.3.5 – If you look closely , you will see that the only difference between these two structures are two occurrences of their operation index, «3» and «4» respectively.

21.3.6 – Withdrawing an abstraction from this set of structures, we obtain:

$$W(\{u_{0_{c3}}, u_{0_{c4}}\}) \to \sigma_{c_U}(p, o)$$

$$: p = \Big\langle \langle «\text{op1}», [\,] \rangle,\ \langle «\text{op2}», [\,] \rangle,\ \langle \langle «\text{result}», \emptyset \rangle, [\cdot] \rangle \Big\rangle$$

$$: o = C_{3_\sigma}\Big(C_{2_\sigma}(«\text{op1}», \rho(«\text{op2}»)),\ C_{2_\sigma}(«\text{op2}», \rho(«\text{op2}»)),$$

$$C_{2_\sigma}(C_{2_\sigma}(«\text{result}», \emptyset), «1») \Big)$$

21.3.7 – This is the equivalent structure, but with the indices removed and replaced with $\emptyset$ to represent that there is no concept in those places.

21.3.8 – We will not give a full account of how this structure is transformed into the configuration in the next section in this work, but we leave the topic with a plausible strategy for obtaining the configurations used in the next section by mechanical processes.

21.4 General Hyperoperation Machine

21.4.1 – Now it's time to build a general hyperoperation machine $\mathcal{M}_{H_x}$.

21.4.2 – This machine first invokes a second machine $\mathcal{M}_{H_c}$ to build a set of configurations that can be executed by $\mathcal{M}_U$ to represent the xth hyperoperation, then evaluates the configurations that it has constructed on-demand with $\mathcal{M}_U$ to obtain results for arbitrary hyperoperational calculations.

21.4.3 – Notice as we work through how we can obtain nearly identical structures to the configurations we build into $\mathcal{M}_U$ by generalizing from the configurations used to evaluate those operations on $\mathcal{M}_U$, including addition and multiplication configurations outlined in §19.

21.4.4 – An important feature of future work will be better-defining these geenralization processes so that there is a fully mechanical description of the process to create a generalized machine from abstracted machine states.

21.4.5 – First, we will define the state specifier for $\mathcal{M}_{H_x}$:

$$\sigma_{H_x}(o_1, o_2, x, c, r) \equiv \Big\langle \langle \text{«op1»}, o_1 \rangle, \ \langle \text{«op2»}, o_2 \rangle, \ \langle \text{«opx»}, x \rangle,$$
$$\langle \text{«configurations»}, c \rangle, \ \langle \text{«result»}, r \rangle \Big\rangle$$

21.4.6 – Here the x parameter is the operation index in H_x.

21.4.7 – We will also need a state specifier for $\mathcal{M}_{H_c}$:

$$\sigma_{H_c}(x, i, s, c) \equiv \Big\langle \langle \text{«opx»}, x \rangle, c \rangle, \ \langle \text{«index»}, i \rangle,$$
$$\langle \text{«state»}, s \rangle, \ \langle \text{«configurations»} \Big\rangle$$
$$\Upsilon(\{\text{«state1»}, \text{«state2»}, \text{«state3»}\}, \text{«state»})$$

21.4.8 – And an associated machine specifier:

$$\mathcal{M}_{H_c}(x) \equiv \sigma_{H_c}(x, \langle \rangle, \text{«0»}, \text{«state1»})$$

21.4.9 – Our first state for $\mathcal{M}_{H_x}$, s_{0_x}, initializes $\mathcal{M}_{H_c}$, and uses its result to set its own «configurations»:

$$s_{0_x} = \sigma_{H_x}([\,], [\,], \text{«not-0»}, [\cdot], [\cdot])$$

$$R(s_{0_x}) \rightarrow \sigma_{H_x}\Big(s_{0_x}[\text{op1}], \ s_{0_x}[\text{op2}], \ s_{0_x}[\text{opx}],$$
$$X\Big(R(\mathcal{M}_{H_c}(s_{0_x}[\text{opx}])), \text{«configurations»} \Big), \ [\,] \Big)$$

21.4.10 – This triggers $\mathcal{M}_{H_c}$, which will build the «configurations» that will be passed to $\mathcal{M}_U$.

21.4.11 – In the coming machines it will be useful to define a specifier σ_{res}:

$$\sigma_{\text{res}}(x) = \langle \text{«result»}, x \rangle$$

21.4.12 – In order to build $\mathcal{M}_{H_c}$, we need to more specifiers that represent the state of the emulated machine, which will execute the actual hyperoperation. The first is a state specifier:

$$\sigma_{H_{op}}(o_1, o_2, x, r) \equiv \Big\langle \langle \text{«op1»}, o_1 \rangle, \ \langle \text{«op2»}, o_2 \rangle, \ \langle \sigma_{\text{res}}(x), r \rangle \Big\rangle$$

21.4.13 – Notice that we are using an unusual pattern to construct the «result» tag using $\sigma_{\text{res}}(x)$. This allows us to parameterize which result type it is based on the index of the hyperoperation.

21.4.14 – We will also need a relation specifier for the emulated machine:

$$\omega_{H_{op}}(o_1, o_2, x, r) \equiv C_{3_\sigma}\Big(C_{2_\sigma}(\text{«op1»}, o_1), \ C_{2_\sigma}(\text{«op2»}, o_2),$$
$$C_{2_\sigma}\big(C_{2_\sigma}(\text{«result»}, x), r\big)\Big)$$

21.4.15 – Let's see the first state of $\mathcal{M}_{H_c}$, which creates a configuration that is the counterpart to the one seen in §21.2.4:

$$s_{1_{H3+}} = \sigma_{H_c}(\text{«3»}, [\,], [\,], \text{«state1»})$$

$$R(s_{1_{H3+}}) \to \sigma_{H_c}\Big(s_{1_{H3+}}[\text{opx}], \ H_0(s_{1_{H3+}}[\text{index}]), \ \text{«state2»},$$
$$T\big(s_{1_{H3+}}[\text{configurations}], \ s_{1_{H3+}}[\text{index}], \ \sigma_{c_U}(p, o)\big)\Big)$$

$$: p = \sigma_{H_{op}}([\,], \ [\,], \ s_{1_{H3+}}[\text{opx}], \ [\cdot])$$
$$: o = \omega_{H_{op}}(\rho(\text{«op1»}), \ \rho(\text{«op2»}), \ s_{1_{H3+}}[\text{opx}], \ \text{«1»})$$

21.4.16 – Note that the T invocation create a new «configuration» for any hyperoperation with the index «3» or greater that sets its «result» to «1».

21.4.17 – The first step of the general case of hyperoperations is general to all cases of $x \geq 3$, but has special cases for $x = 2$ and $x = 1$ below.

21.4.18 – This rule creates a new «configuration» in $s_{1_{H3+}}[\text{configurations}]$ at index $s_{1_{H3+}}[\text{index}]$.

21.4.19 – The pattern that determines when this rule applies is $\sigma_{H_{op}}([\,],[\,],s_{1_{H3+}}[\text{opx}],[\cdot])$.

21.4.20 – $\omega_{H_{op}}(\rho(«\text{op1}»),\ \rho(«\text{op2}»),\ s_{1_{H3+}}[\text{opx}],\ «1»)$ indicates the operation of the configuration. In this case, that equates to initializing the hyperoperation's result to «1» (which is the first step for all cases where the hyperoperation index is 3 or greater).

21.4.21 – $H_0(s_{1_{H3+}}[\text{index}])$ increments the index so that the next configuration will be written after this one.

21.4.22 – And finally, «state2» defines the next state of our configuration-building machine $\mathcal{M}_{H_c}$.

21.4.23 – One thing to pay attention to is when we use $s_{1_{H3+}}[\text{opx}]$ to "statically" embed the index of the hyperoperation we're currently defining. This is because we iteratively define the largest-indexed hyperoperation, then the next-largest, all the way down to H_1.

21.4.24 – In the next state, very similar to the above but only when $x = 2$—as in multiplication—the initial value of «result» is «0».

21.4.25 – This configuration is nearly identical to its counterpart in §19.11.5:

$$s_{1_{H2}} = \sigma_{H_c}(«2»,[\,],[\,],«\text{state1}»)$$

$$R(s_{1_{H2}}) \to \sigma_{H_c}\Big(s_{1_{H2}}[\text{opx}],\ H_0(s_{1_{H2}}[\text{index}]),\ «\text{state2}»,$$
$$T(s_{1_{H2}}[\text{configurations}],\ s_{1_{H2}}[\text{index}],\ \sigma_{c_U}(p,o))\Big)$$

$$: p = \sigma_{H_{op}}([\,],\ [\,],\ s_{1_{H2}}[\text{opx}],\ [\cdot])$$
$$: o = \omega_{H_{op}}(\rho(«\text{op1}»),\ \rho(«\text{op2}»),\ s_{1_{H2}}[\text{opx}],\ «0»)\Big)$$

21.4.26 – And in the case that $x = 1$, as in addition, its initial value is «op1», the analogue of §19.11.11:

$$s_{1_{H1}} = \sigma_{H_c}(\text{«1»}, [\,], [\,], \text{«state1»})$$

$$R(s_{1_{H1}}) \to \sigma_{H_c}\Big(s_{1_{H1}}[\text{opx}],\ H_0(s_{1_{H1}}[\text{index}]),\ \text{«state2»},$$
$$T(s_{1_{H1}}[\text{configurations}],\ s_{1_{H1}}[\text{index}],\ \sigma_{c_U}(p, o))\Big)$$

$$: p = \sigma_{H_{op}}([\,], [\,], s_{1_{H1}}[\text{opx}], [\cdot])$$
$$: o = \omega_{H_{op}}(\rho(\text{«op1»}),\ \rho(\text{«op2»}),\ s_{1_{H1}}[\text{opx}],\ \rho(\text{«op1»}))$$

21.4.27 – Now we need to create a configuration that will execute the repeated operation.

21.4.28 – In order to make our work more legible, we'll define a special version of ρ, ρ_{res}, which allows us to create parameterized «result» objects based on the needed hyperoperation index:

$$\rho_{\text{res}}(x) \equiv \rho(\langle\text{«result»}, x\rangle)$$

21.4.29 – And an operation specifier H_{x_σ}:

$$H_{x_\sigma}(x) \equiv X_\sigma(R_\sigma(r),\ \sigma_{\text{res}}(H_0^{-1}(x)))$$

$$: r = \omega_{H_{op}}(\rho(\text{«op1»}),\ \rho_{\text{res}}(x),\ H_0^{-1}(x),\ [\,])$$

21.4.30 – This operation specifier evaluates the next-indexed hyperoperation from the passed x.

21.4.31 – Notice that $\rho_{\text{res}}(x)$ gets the next-indexed «result», e.g. «result3» in the case of that $x = 4$.

21.4.32 – Below is the state in the general case that $x \geq 2$. ($x = 1$ needs to explicitly invoke H_0.) This is the analogue of the configuration defined in §19.11.7 for multiplication:

$$s_{2_{H2+}} = \sigma_{H_c}(\text{«2»}, [\,], [\,], \text{«state2»})$$

$$R(s_{2_{H2+}}) \rightarrow \sigma_{H_c}\Big(s_{2_{H2+}}[\text{opx}], \ H_0(s_{2_{H2+}}[\text{index}]), \ \text{«state3»},$$
$$T(s_{2_{H2+}}[\text{configurations}], \ s_{2_{H2+}}[\text{index}], \ \sigma_{c_U}(p,o))\Big)$$

$$: p = \sigma_{H_{op}}([\,], \ [\,], \ s_{2_{H2+}}[\text{opx}], \ [\cdot])$$
$$: o = \omega_{H_{op}}(\rho(\text{«op1»}), \ H_{0_\sigma}^{-1}(\rho(\text{«op2»})), \ s_{2_{H2+}}[\text{opx}], \ H_{x_\sigma}(s_{2_{H2+}}[\text{opx}]))$$

21.4.33 – Be aware of the usage of H_{x_σ}, defined above, to evaluate the next-indexed hyperoperation.

21.4.34 – That operation specifier allows us to recursively call down to the next hyperoperation and retrieve its results.

21.4.35 – Now we construct the configuration for the special case that $x = 1$, i.e. addition.

21.4.36 – In this case we do not call the same machine recursively, but instead utilize H_0 directly via H_{0_σ}:

$$s_{2_{H1}} = \sigma_{H_c}(\text{«1»}, [\,], [\,], \text{«state2»})$$

$$R(s_{2_{H1}}) \rightarrow \sigma_{H_c}\Big(s_{2_{H1}}[\text{opx}], \ H_0(s_{2_{H1}}[\text{index}]), \ \text{«state3»},$$
$$T(s_{2_{H1}}[\text{configurations}], \ s_{2_{H1}}[\text{index}], \ \sigma_{c_U}(p,o))\Big)$$

$$: p = \sigma_{H_{op}}([\,], \ [\,], \ s_{2_{H1}}[\text{opx}], \ [\cdot])$$
$$: o = \omega_{H_{op}}(\rho(\text{«op1»}), \ H_{0_\sigma}^{-1}(\rho(\text{«op2»})), \ s_{2_{H1}}[\text{opx}], \ H_{0_\sigma}(\rho_{\text{res}}(s_{2_{H1}}[\text{opx}])))$$

21.4.37 – In $\mathcal{M}_{H_c}$'s final state, we construct for each hyperoperation's "cleanup state," in which we set «op1» and «op2» to [ ], we decrement «opx» to generate the state for the next hoperoperation, and we set the configuration-generating machine's state back to «state1» to renew the cycle.

$$\mathcal{M}_{H_x}$$

$$s_{0_{Hx}} \longrightarrow \mathcal{M}_{H_c} \longrightarrow s_{1_{Hx}} \longrightarrow \mathcal{M}_U \longrightarrow \text{end}$$

Figure 46: M_{H_x} *State Graph:* The initial state of M_{H_x}, $s_{0_{Hx}}$, sends the input to M_{H_c}. M_{H_c} constructs a set of «configurations» that can be evaluated by $\mathcal{M}_U$. $s_{1_{Hx}}$ sets the «structure» of $\mathcal{M}_U$ given the input of M_{H_x} and evaluates $\mathcal{M}_U$ with the set of «configurations» generated by M_{H_c}.

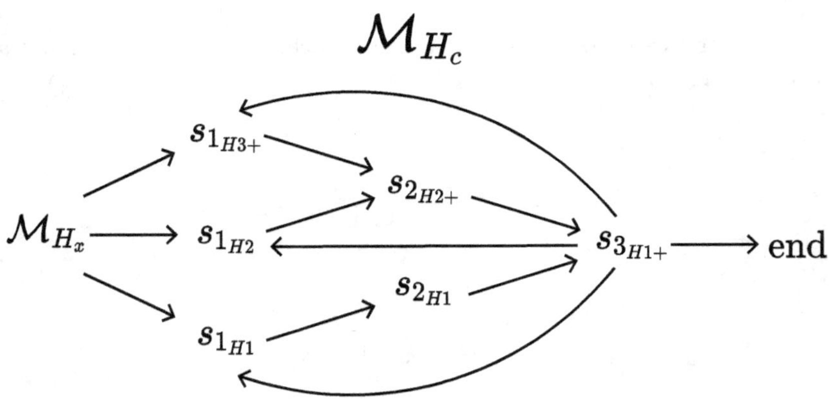

Figure 47: M_{H_c} *State Graph:* Each s_1 creates the initial state of the machine for the current hyperoperation, each s_2 creates the state that repeats the next hyperoperation, and the shared s_3 will cycle back to the next s_1 if the hyperoperation index is less than «1» or will end otherwise. Notice that s_1 has two special cases for how to initialize the machine, s_2 has only one special case for when H_1 needs to invoke H_0, and s_3 has no special cases.

$$s_{3_{H1+}} = \sigma_{H_c}(\text{«not-0»}, [\,], [\,], \text{«state3»})$$

$$R(s_{3_{H1+}}) \to \sigma_{H_c}\Big(s_{3_{H1+}}[\text{opx}],\ H_0(s_{3_{H1+}}[\text{index}]),\ \text{«state1»},$$
$$T\big(s_{3_{H1+}}[\text{configurations}],\ s_{3_{H1+}}[\text{index}],\ \sigma_{c_U}(p, o)\big)\Big)$$

$$: p = \sigma_{H_{op}}([\,],\ \text{«}\dot{0}\text{»},\ s_{3_{H1+}}[\text{opx}],\ [\,])$$
$$: o = \omega_{H_{op}}([\,],\ [\,],\ s_{3_{H1+}}[\text{opx}],\ \rho_{\text{res}}(s_{3_{H1+}}[\text{opx}]))$$

21.4.38 – $\mathcal{M}_{H_c}$ is now complete. The final remaining step is to add a state to $\mathcal{M}_{H_x}$ that uses the configurations that have been set by $\mathcal{M}_{H_c}$ to invoke $\mathcal{M}_U$ and execute the hyperoperation we constructed:

$$s_{1_x} = \sigma_{H_x}([\,], [\,], [\,], [\,], [\cdot])$$

$$R(s_{1_x}) \to \sigma_{H_x}\Big([\,],\ [\,],\ [\,],\ [\,],\ X(m[\text{«result»}], \sigma_{\text{res}}(s_{1_x}[\text{opx}]))\Big)$$

$$: m = \mathcal{M}_U(o,\ s_{1_x}[\text{configurations}])$$
$$: o = \sigma_{H_{op}}(s_{1_x}[\text{op1}], s_{1_x}[\text{op2}], s_{1_x}[\text{opx}], [\,])$$

21.4.39 – Finally, we define our operation H_x:

$$H_x(o_1, o_2, x) \equiv X(R(\mathcal{M}_{H_x}(o_1, o_2, x)), \text{«result»})$$

21.4.40 – And now we can see the results of our generalized hyperoperation machine:

$$H_x(\text{«1»}, \text{«6»}, \text{«1»}) = \text{«7»}$$
$$H_x(\text{«4»}, \text{«3»}, \text{«2»}) = \text{«12»}$$
$$H_x(\text{«2»}, \text{«3»}, \text{«3»}) = \text{«8»}$$
$$H_x(\text{«2»}, \text{«4»}, \text{«4»}) = \text{«65536»}$$

22 Toward Intelligence

"I do really believe that creativity is computational."

—Yoshua Bengio

This concluding outline examines how our work thus far can be pushed forward, and sets a direction for future inquiry into mechanical "intelligence."

22.1 What Is Intelligence?

22.1.1 – Intelligence is the ability to create and execute arbitrary cognitive mechanisms as required for the purpose of meeting new tasks and challenges.

22.1.2 – In order to instantiate anything deserving of the label "intelligence," we will need to make progress along multiple courses.

22.1.3 – To conclude our inquiry, we'll outline three specific areas as parts of a program for future research, and finally illustrate a direction for we may connect them to create intelligent machines.

22.2 Perceptual Operations

22.2.1 – The machines we've constructed in this book—being primarily abstract mathematical and computational in nature—have not demanded that we have any thorough formulation of outside circumstances.

22.2.2 – In most cases, an intelligent machine adapts to the needs of its present situation in its environment. That adaptation requires environmental input—in our case in the form of perceptions.

22.2.3 – Though we gave broad definitions of I and G—in §5.4.2 and §7.2.3, respectively—there is much detail to be added in the case of an actionable mechanical system.

22.2.4 – In the case of G, the primary challenge is to determine a suitable representation of the perception in the terms of manifestations, likely in terms of some sparse structure.

22.2.5 – For I, we then need to take that sparse representation and build from it a complex conceptual structure that models the machine's environment.

22.2.6 – This environment need not necessarily be physical. We could imagine machines that live in virtual worlds—which may be created to have some emulated properties of our world, but may also live in an entirely abstract environments of information, mathematical structures, etc.

22.2.7 – This conceptual model is critical to determining how the machine acts on its environment.

22.3 Goals

22.3.1 – In order to determine how it will act on the environment, the machine needs to formulate a goal—an internal model of a desired end state of the environment.

22.3.2 – I think we can be fairly certain that this model will also be in the form of a conceptual structure.

22.3.3 – So the optimal machine will turn perceptions into a model of the world. It will then use that model to formulate its version of a desired alternate state of the model, and then determine an efficient set of actions that will lead to the highest expectation in terms of matching future perceptions to its model of the desired state.

22.3.4 – In the most autonomous systems, goals cause the production of sub-goals, which can have their own sub-goals, and so-on.

22.3.5 – Let's take the task of putting a ball through a hoop as an example. At minimum, the mind needs the following to decide on a course of action:

1. A conceptual model of the ball;
2. A conceptual model of the hoop;
3. A conceptual model of the ball on one side of the hoop;
4. A conceptual model of the ball on the other side of the hoop (i.e. the goal);
5. Some machine that goes about modeling the transformation from the first state to the second one, in different iterations, if needed; and
6. Some mechanism that determines whether one transformation is superior to the others.

22.3.6 – Once we have a properly formulated way to model the environment of the machine in terms of conceptual structures, we will have made a large step towards fitting the machine with goals that match our own.

22.4 Abstraction Optimization

22.4.1 – The recursion of goals created by the system ultimately has its roots in the system of abstraction it uses.

22.4.2 – For example, if a machine was set with a goal of performing calculations of hyperoperations it was given examples of, the machine would start by formulating individual machines for special cases, and an ideal machine would take those separate special-case machines and abstract away the states of $\mathcal{M}_{H_x}$, defined in §21.

22.4.3 – The formulations of Υ^* (and W, by its usage of Υ^*) in this book are ad hoc and extremely computationally inefficient. This is a rich area for future study, especially in producing heuristics and more efficient algorithms for determining good abstractions.

22.5 Discrete & Non-Discrete Approaches

22.5.1 – Though the present landscape of machine learning is dominated by the recent success of deep learning techniques, I believe that ultimately the combination of discrete (structural and symbolic), network, statistical, and Bayesian approaches ones will yield the most productive results.

22.5.2 – A specific area that I believe is ripe for research is the emergence of statistical phenomena out of discrete ones and vice versa.

22.5.3 – Even deep learning algorithms, which are ostensibly non-discrete in nature, are implemented on discrete machines.

22.5.4 – I suspect that conceptual machines built with stochastic state transitions, mentioned in passing in §12, might have properties that begin to resemble some features of these other non-discrete approaches. These features may be particularly useful in the "lower" levels of the mechanical hierarchy, especially with respect to where neural nets have seen the most success in applications today: in the analysis of primary "perceptual" input, specifically in auditory and visual pattern recognition.

22.5.5 – In the other directions, some progress in the formulation of discrete representations in non-discrete systems would result in huge breakthroughs.

22.5.6 – The notions of synthesis between discrete and non-discrete approaches to machine intelligence will need to find more attention.

22.6 An Intelligent Machine

22.6.1 – An intelligent machine requires a way of translating perceptions into conceptual structures; it needs the ability to manipulate that structure; it must be able to compare it to another structure that represents some desired state (i.e. a goal); and it must be able to produce an action which is likely to lead to the desired state, given its input.

22.6.2 – Our model of an intelligent machine $\mathcal{M}_i$ is given with an experience χ, which is interpreted into a conceptual structure with operation I.

22.6.3 – The workings of I must take into account k, a set of the existing conceptual structures that constitute the machine's knowledge, and the resulting structure of $I(\chi \mid k)$ can then be added back into k.

22.6.4 – $G(\chi \mid k)$ may also have its results added to k.

22.6.5 – The result of $I(\chi \mid k)$ is e, the machine's model of its environment:

$$I(\chi \mid k) \to e$$
$$k' = k \cup \{e, G(\chi \mid k)\}$$

$$\mathcal{M}_i$$

$$k \downarrow$$

$$\chi \to I(\chi \mid k) \to e \to \mathcal{M}_a(e, g) \to c$$

$$\downarrow \qquad \uparrow$$

$$\mathcal{M}_g(e) \to g$$

Figure 48: $\mathcal{M}_i$ *State Graph:* This graph shows the interaction of each machine and operation within $\mathcal{M}_i$ from input χ to output c.

22.6.6 – We assume the machine $\mathcal{M}_i$ to have a submachine, $\mathcal{M}_g$, which takes a model of an environment and formulates a goal g:

$$R(\mathcal{M}_g(e)) \to g$$

22.6.7 – A machine $\mathcal{M}_a$ accepts e and g as input, and produces a set of «configurations» c that can be executed by $\mathcal{M}_U$ to produce g as the «result»:

$$R(\mathcal{M}_a(e, g)) \to c$$

22.6.8 – Plausible implementations of $\mathcal{M}_a$ could use W to withdraw a common structure from e and g, applying heuristics and stochastic exploration to find solutions to the conversion of e to g, given that common structure.

22.6.9 – The solution c represents the action required to reach state g from e; c is the result of $\mathcal{M}_i$, along with the updated state of knowledge k'.

22.6.10 – $\mathcal{M}_a$ may construct intermediate goals, and may invoke itself with those intermediate goals to build the set of configurations c.

22.6.11 – From the highest level:

$$R(\mathcal{M}_i(\chi \mid k)) \to \big\langle \langle \text{«configurations»}, c \rangle, \ \langle \text{«knowledge»}, k' \rangle \big\rangle$$

22.6.12 – Finally, to enact the solution:

$$U(e, c) \to g$$

References

Brown, Cecil H. 1999. *Lexical acculturation in native american languages.* Oxford, United Kingdom: Oxford University Press.

Clayton, Ewan. 2019. Where did writing begin? https://www.bl.uk/ history-of-writing/articles/where-did-writing-begin (29 January, 2021).

Dufour, Robert & Judith F. Kroll. 1995. Matching words to concepts in two languages: A test of the concept mediation model of bilingual representation. *Memory & Cognition.*

Duncan, Hilary D., Jim Nikelski, Randi Pilon, Jason Steffener, Howard Chertkow & Natalie A. Phillips. 2018. Structural brain differences between monolingual and multilingual patients with mild cognitive impairment and alzheimer disease: Evidence for cognitive reserve. *Neuropsychologia* 109, 270–282. doi:https: //doi.org/10.1016/j.neuropsychologia.2017.12.036. https://www. sciencedirect.com/science/article/pii/S0028393217305109.

Haines, Francis. 1928. *Where did the plains indians get their horses?* Arlington, Virginia: American Anthropological Association.

Hall, Wyatte C. 2017. What you don't know can hurt you: The risk of language deprivation by impairing sign language development in deaf children. *Maternal and Child Health Journal.*

Howell, James. 1997. *Essential chess endings: The tournament player's guide.* London, United Kingdom: Bratsford.

Johansson, Fredrik, Dan-Anders Jirenhed, Anders Rasmussen, Riccardo Zucca & Germund Hesslow. 2014. Memory trace and timing mechanism localized to cerebellar purkinje cells. *Proceedings of the National Academy of Sciences* 111(41), 14930–14934. doi:10.1073/pnas.1415371111. https://www.pnas.org/doi/abs/10.1073/ pnas.1415371111.

Klima, Edward S. & Ursula Bellugi. 1979. *The signs of language.* Harvard University Press.

Morin, Alain, Bob Uttl & Breanne Hamper. 2011. Self-reported frequency, content, and functions of inner speech. *Procedia - Social and Behavioral Sciences* 30, 1714–1718. doi:https://doi.org/10.1016/j. sbspro.2011.10.331. https://www.sciencedirect.com/science/article/pii/

S1877042811021562.

Pepperberg, Irene M. 1994. Numerical competence in an african gray parrot (psittacus erithacus). *Journal of Comparative Psychology* 108, 36–44.

Roser, Max & Esteban Ortiz-Ospina. 2013. Literacy. https:// ourworldindata.org/literacy (29 January, 2021).

Senghas, Ann & Marie Coppola. 2001. Children creating language: How nicaraguan sign language acquired a spatial grammar. *Psychological Science* 12(4), 323–328. doi:10.1111/1467-9280.00359. %0Ahttps://doi.org/ 10.1111/1467-9280.00359%0A%0A.

Shannon, Claude Elwood. 1948. A mathematical theory of communication. *The Bell System Technical Journal* 27, 379–423. http://plan9.bell-labs. com/cm/ms/what/shannonday/shannon1948.pdf (22 April, 2003).

Stroop, John Ridley. 1935. Studies of inference in serial verbal reactions. *Journal of Experimental Psychology.*

Tomonaga, Masaki & Tetsuro Matsuzawa. 2002. Enumeration of briefly presented items by the chimpanzee (pan troglodytes) and humans (homo sapiens). *Animal Learning & Behavior* 30, 143–157. doi:https://doi.org/10.3758/BF03192916. https://link.springer.com/ article/10.3758/BF03192916.

Turing, Alan M. 1936. On computable numbers, with an application to the Entscheidungsproblem. *Proceedings of the London Mathematical Society* 2(42), 230–265. http://www.cs.helsinki.fi/u/gionis/cc05/ OnComputableNumbers.pdf.